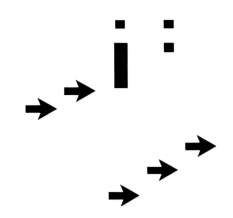

8
4   EUROPEAN   PHOTOGRAPHY

                        8
                        3

EDITED   BY,   EDITÉ   PAR,   HERAUSGEGEBEN   VON

EDWARD   BOOTH-CLIBBORN

THE   THIRD   ANNUAL   OF   EUROPEAN   EDITORIAL,   BOOK

POSTER,   ADVERTISING   AND   UNPUBLISHED   PHOTOGRAPHY

LE   TROISIÈME   ANNUAIRE   EUROPÉEN   DE   PHOTOGRAPHIES

DE   PRESSE,   DU   LIVRE,   DE   L'AFFICHE,   DE   LA   PUBLICITÉ

ET   D'OEUVRES   NON   PUBLIÉES

DAS   DRITTE   JAHRBUCH   DER   EUROPÄISCHEN   REDAKTIONS-

BUCH-,   PLAKAT-,   WERBE-   UND   UNVERÖFFENTLICHTEN

FOTOGRAFIE

EUROPEAN   PHOTOGRAPHY

12   CARLTON   HOUSE   TERRACE   LONDON

Book designed by Nicholas Thirkell & Partners Limited.

Editorial production: Lorena Kempff.

The exhibition of the photography in this book will be shown at The National Film Theatre, London.

The captions and photography in this book have been supplied by the entrants. Whilst every effort has been made to ensure accuracy, European Photography do not, under any circumstances, accept responsibility for errors or omissions.

No part of this book may be reproduced in any manner whatsoever without written permission.

Cover photograph by Barney Edwards

Photographs of the Jury by Rolph Gobits

Maquettistes du livre Nicholas Thirkell & Partners Limited.

Rédactrice du texte: Lorena Kempff.

L'exposition d'oeuvres d'art de ce livre aura lieu à The National Film Theatre, Londres.

Les légendes et les oeuvres d'art figurant dans ce livre ont été fournies par les personnes inscrites. Bien que tout ait été fait pour en assurer l'exactitude European Photography n'accepte aucune responsabilité en cas d'erreurs ou d'omissions.

Aucune partie de ce livre ne peut être reproduite en aucune façon sans autorisation écrite.

Photographie de couverture par Barney Edwards.

Photographies du Jury par Rolph Gobits

Buch gestaltet von Nicholas Thirkell & Partners Limited.

Textredaktion: Lorena Kempff.

Die Ausstellung der in diesem Buch gezeigten Fotos findet statt im National Film Theatre, London.

Die textlichen Angaben zu den Abbildungen und die Vorlagen dazu wurden uns von den Einsendern zur Verfügung gestellt. Der genauen Wiedergabe wurde größte Sorgfalt gewidmet; European Photography kann jedoch unter keinen Umständen die Verantwortung für Fehler oder Auslassungen übernehmen.

Die Wiedergabe dieses Buches vollständig oder in Auszügen in jedweder Form ist ohne schriftliche Genehmigung nicht gestattet.

Umschlag-Foto von Barney Edwards.

Fotos der Jury von Rolph Gobits

European Photography Call for Entries Copyright ©1983

The following companies hold the exclusive distribution rights for European Photography 83/84:

France: Sofédis, Paris

USA/Canada: Harry N Abrams Inc., New York
ISBN 0-8109-0870-0

UK: Devonshire House, 29 Elmfield Road, Bromley, Kent BR1 1LT
Tel: 01-290 6611

Rest of the world:
Fleetbooks, 100 Park Avenue, New York, NY 10017

Printed in Japan by Dai Nippon. Paper: 157 GSM coated
Typeface: News Gothic
Filmset by: Filmcomposition, London

Published by Fleetbooks S.A. Switzerland
Copyright ©1983.

EDWARD BOOTH-CLIBBORN

There must, today, be many millions of cameras in use all over the world. Some of them are in the hands of good photographers. Only a handful of them are the tools of really great photographers.

But then, as in all the visual arts and other walks of life, greatness is a rare quality.

Often, it's the result of some natural talent. More often, it's a combination of talent, training and the sheer force of mind that stems from individuality.

In the main then, the truly great photographers are those who, with the technical knowledge to back them, have a different angle on life; a purely personal point of view.

Within the pages of this book you will see, as in previous editions of European Photography, the work of some great photographers.

For the most part, their work has been done for the editors of magazines and newspapers, covering the explosive events of the world as news, illustrating the passive side of life as features.

And what a world these photographs show us! It seems, from many of the images here, to be a world in uproar; a place where guns are worn as handbags, where even the crazy no longer inflict any shock.

The stark realism of some of the work in this book serves, through its detached, almost impersonal point of view, to make us even more aware of the subjects and their lives than would any image contrived or pulled together to shock for the sake of shock. Their reality excludes the possibility of misunderstanding.

Yet for all that many of these images have a quality of "I-want-you-to-look-at-this-just-as-it-is", the majority of them are superbly composed. As such, they are the work of photographers whose command of their equipment is more than matched by their pictorial sense and their knowledge of composition.

I'm glad to say that the same degree of technical expertise matched to a seeing eye can still be found among photographers who work in the advertising area.

One of them – Barney Edwards – has a particularly appealing set of pictures in the Unpublished Section of this edition of European Photography. Best known for his effective work for some of London's leading advertising agencies (he has photographed Range Rovers, Sandhurst Chapel War Memorial, Chris Bonnington and his Olympus camera and, for Johnnie Walker Black Label, a superbly dramatic North Sea sunset) he has, in his spare time, created a remarkable series of flower pictures. With their simple, uncluttered compositions they are, to me, comparable with many of the fine Old Masters' paintings of flowers, and equally rewarding.

I hope you will enjoy this edition of European Photography and find something in it that's rewarding to you. And I hope too that, if you are interested in photography as an art or craft, the work you will find here will stimulate your mind – and eye – so that, by learning from some of the great practitioners of our time, you will be able to aspire to your own level of greatness, by adopting your own point of view and your own angle on life.

Il doit y avoir aujourd'hui des millions d'appareils photographiques utilisés à travers le monde. Quelques-uns se trouvent entre les mains de bons photographes. Une poignée d'entre eux seulement sont les outils de travail de vraiment grands photographes.

Mais bien sûr, comme dans tous les arts visuels et autres champs d'activités, la grandeur est une qualité rare.

Souvent c'est le résultat d'un talent naturel. Plus souvent c'est une association de talent, d'entraînement et de pure volonté d'esprit qui provient d'individualité.

En général donc, les vraiment grands photographes sont ceux qui, soutenus par une connaissance technique, ont une vision différente sur la vie, un point de vue purement personnel.

Dans les pages de ce livre vous verrez, comme dans les éditions précédentes de European Photography, le travail de quelques grands photographes.

Pour la plupart, leur travail a été créé pour les éditeurs de magazines et journaux, couvrant les événements explosifs au monde en actualités, montrant le côté passif de la vie en articles.

Et quel monde nous montrent ces photographies! Il semble, d'après ces images que c'est un monde en tumulte; un endroit où les fusils se portent en bagages, où même les fous ne causent plus de choc.

Le réalisme absolu de quelques oeuvres dans ce livre sert, par son point de vue détaché, presqu'impersonnel, à nous rendre encore plus conscients des sujets et de leur vie que ne le ferait une image inventée ou construite avec l'idée de créer la stupéfaction. Leur réalité exclut toute possibilité de malentendu.

Toutefois, pour autant que ces images aient une qualité de "je-veux-que-vous-voyiez-ceci-tel-que-c'est", la majorité d'entre elles sont superbement composées. Ainsi, elles sont l'oeuvre de photographes qui ont une commande de leur équipement plus qu'égalée par leur sens de l'image et leur connaissance de la composition.

Je suis heureux de pouvoir dire qu'on trouve encore le même degré d'expertise technique assorti d'un coup d'oeil pour la vérité chez quelques photographes qui travaillent dans le domaine de la publicité.

Un d'eux – Barney Edwards – a une série d'images particulièrement attachantes dans la section des photos non publiées dans cette édition de European Photography. Surtout connu par son travail frappant pour les principales agences publicitaires de Londres (Il a photographié les Range Rovers, le War Memorial de la Chapelle de Sandhurst, Chris Bonnington et son appareil Olympus, et pour Johnnie Walker Black Label, un coucher de soleil dramatique sur la Mer du Nord) il a, dans son temps libre, créé une série remarquable d'images de fleurs. Par leur composition simple et nette elles sont pour moi, comparables aux peintures de fleurs des maîtres anciens, et me font le même effet.

J'espère que vous aimerez cette édition de European Photography et que vous y trouverez un apport certain. Et j'espère aussi, si vous vous intéressez à la photographie comme art ou métier d'art, que le travail que vous verrez ici vous stimulera l'esprit – et l'oeil – et vous permettra, instruit par les grands interprètes de notre époque, d'aspirer à votre propre niveau de grandeur, en adoptant votre propre point de vue et votre propre vision sur la vie.

Es müssen heutzutage überall in der Welt etliche Millionen Kameras im Gebrauch sein. Einige befinden sich in den Händen guter Photographen; nur eine Handvoll sind Instrumente wirklich großer Photographen.

Denn Größe ist, wie in allen visuellen Künsten und anderen Lebenswegen, eine rare Qualität.

Oft ist sie das Ergebnis eines natürlichen Talents; des öfteren eine Kombination von Talent, Training und purer Willensstärke, geboren aus der Individualität.

Die Mehrzahl der wirklich großen Photographen sind diejenigen, die, über das technische Können hinaus, dem Leben gegenüber einen ganz besonderen Gesichtspunkt haben, einen ganz persönlichen Standpunkt vertreten.

Auf den Seiten dieses Buches, wie in vorherigen Ausgaben der European Photography, werden Sie die Arbeiten einiger großer Photographen sehen.

Zum größten Teil entstanden ihre Arbeiten im Auftrag von Zeitschrifts- und Zeitungsredakteuren, in der Form von Nachrichtenmaterial über die explosiven Ereignisse der Welt, oder als Reportage über die passive Seite des Lebens.

Und welch eine Welt uns die Photos zeigen! Viele der hier gezeigten Bilder scheinen von einer Welt im Aufruhr zu zeugen; einer Welt, in der Waffen als Handtaschen getragen werden und in der selbst Verrückte keinerlei Schock mehr hervorrufen.

Der nackte Realismus einiger der Arbeiten in diesem Buch, durch seinen distanzierten, fast unpersönlichen Standpunkt, steigert unser Bewußtsein gegenüber den Objekten und deren Lebensweise eher als jedes Bild, das des puren Schocks wegen erfunden oder zusammengestellt wurde. Diese Realität schließt jegliche Möglichkeit des Misverständnisses aus.

Dennoch, obwohl viele dieser Bilder eine Qualität von "Sehen-Sie-es-sich-genauso-an-wie-es-ist" beinhalten, sind die meisten hervorragende Kompositionen. Es sind die Arbeiten von Photographen, deren Beherrschung ihrer technischen Ausstattung noch übertroffen wird von ihrem bildlichen Einfühlungs-vermögen und ihrem Können im Bereich der Komposition.

Es freut mich, daß der gleiche Grad von technischem Können, zusammen mit einem sehenden Auge, auch unter Photographen zu finden ist, die in der Werbung arbeiten.

Von einem von ihnen – Barney Edwards – erscheint eine besonders attraktive Serie von Photos innerhalb der Kategorie Unveröffentliche Arbeiten in dieser Ausgabe der European Photography. Obwohl eher bekannt für seine eindrucksvollen Arbeiten im Auftrag einiger der führenden Werbeagenturen Londons (für die er zum Beispiel Range Rovers, die Sandhurst Chapel Kriegsgedenkstätte, Chris Bonnington mit seiner Olympus Kamera und für Johnnie Walker Black Label einen hervorragend dramatischen Sonnenuntergang in der Nordsee photographierte), hat er in seiner Freizeit eine bemerkenswerte Serie von Blumenbildern geschaffen. Diese simplen, unverfälsch-ten Kompositionen sind meiner Meinung nach vergleichbar mit den Blumen-Malereien der alten Künstler und ebenso reichhaltig.

Ich hoffe, Sie werden diese Ausgabe der European Photography genießen und auf ihren Seiten irgend etwas finden, das für Sie belohnend ist. Ebenso hoffe ich, daß, wenn Sie Interesse haben an der Kunst oder dem Können der Photographie, diese Arbeiten Ihre Empfindung – und Ihr Auge – bereichern, so daß das Vorbild einiger der großen Praktiker der heutigen Zeit Sie vielleicht dazu verleitet, Ihren eigenen Standpunkt, Ihren persönlichen Gesichtspunkt zu finden und dadurch Ihren eigenen Grad der Größe zu erstreben.

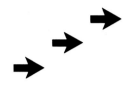

NEIL GODFREY

Neil Godfrey studied illustration at Sheffield College of Art from 1953 to 1956, and graphic design at the Royal College of Art from 1958 to 1961. Since 1961 he has worked as Art Director for Doyle Dane Bernbach Ltd, New York and London, and as Art Director at Wells Rich Greene and at Collett Dickenson Pearce & Partners. His work has won a number of international awards.

Neil Godfrey a étudié l'illustration au Sheffield College of Art de 1953 à 1956, et le design graphique au Royal College of Art de 1958 à 1961. Depuis 1961 il a travaillé comme Directeur Artistique pour Doyle Dane Bernbach Ltd, à New York et Londres, et comme Directeur Artistique chez Wells Rich Greene et chez Collett Dickenson Pearce & Partners. Son travail lui a valu nombre de prix internationaux.

Von 1953 bis 1956 studierte Neil Godfrey Illustration am Sheffield College of Art, und graphische Kunst am Londoner Royal College of Art von 1958 bis 1961. Seit 1961 war er für Doyle Dane Bernbach Ltd in New York und London als Art Direktor tätig; später wurde er Art Direktor bei Wells Rich Greene und Collett Dickenson Pearce & Partners. Mehrere seiner Arbeiten erhielten internationale Auszeichnungen.

J E A N - P I E R R E   M O N T A I G N E

Jean-Pierre Montaigne studied advertising at the Ecole des Métiers d'Art in Paris, and then went on to work as a designer on several publications. In 1969 he created the visuals of "Zoom," of which he became the Art Director until 1974, when he started working for the monthly "Réalités." For eight years now he has been the Art Director of "L'Expansion," the leading economy journal in France.

Jean-Pierre Montaigne a étudié la publicité à l'Ecole des Métiers d'Art à Paris, et a travaillé ensuite comme designer pour plusieurs publications. En 1969 il a créé la section visuelle de "Zoom" dont il est devenu Directeur Artistique jusqu'en 1974, date à laquelle il a

commencé à travailler pour le mensuel "Réalités." Depuis huit ans il est Directeur Artistique de "l'Expansion," la principale publication économique en France.

Nach einem Studium der Werbung an der Ecole des Métiers d'Art in Paris arbeitete Jean-Pierre Montaigne als Designer an verschiedenen Veröffentlichungen. 1969 schuf er den visuellen Stil der Zeitschrift "Zoom," war dort Art Direktor bis 1974 und ging danach zur Monatszeitschrift "Réalités." Seit acht Jahren ist er Art Direktor des führenden Wirtschafts-Journals in Frankreich, "L'Expansion."

ROBERT PRIEST

Robert Priest is Art Director of "Newsweek Magazine," New York. He was previously Art Director of "Esquire Magazine" in New York, "Weekend Magazine" in Toronto, of "Radio Times" in London, and of other periodicals. His work has won major awards in New York, London and Toronto. A member of several design and illustration juries in Europe and North America, he was recently Chairman of the American Institute of Graphic Arts.

Robert Priest est Directeur Artistique de "Newsweek Magazine," New York. Il a précédemment été Directeur Artistique d' "Esquire" à New York, de "Weekend Magazine" à Toronto, de "Radio Times" à Londres, et d'autres périodiques. Son travail a été récompensé par d'importants prix à New York, Londres et Toronto. Membre de plusieurs jurys de design et d'illustration en Europe et en Amerique du Nord, il était, récemment, President de l'American Institute of Graphic Arts.

Robert Priest ist Art Direktor beim "Newsweek Magazine" in New York. Zuvor war er als Art Direktor bei "Esquire Magazine" in New York, bei "Weekend Magazine" in Toronto, bei "Radio Times" in London und anderen Zeitschriften tätig. Seine Arbeit hat ihm mehrere Auszeichnungen in New York, London und Toronto eingebracht. Er ist Mitglied mehrerer Gestaltungs- und Illustrations-Jurys und wurde vor kurzem zum Präsidenten des American Institute of Graphic Arts bestellt.

MICHAEL RAND

Michael Rand studied at Goldsmiths College of Art. He worked as a freelance designer before joining Beaverbrook Newspapers as consultant designer to the "Daily Express," where he pioneered the use of diagrams and charts illustrating the daily news in graphic form. In 1963 he became Art Editor of the "Sunday Times Magazine." He then for a short time became Design Director and Associate Editor of the "Sunday Times." However, he returned to the "Sunday Times Magazine" as Art Director and Managing Editor. He has won many awards for art direction, including D&AD Silver and Gold Awards.

Michael Rand a fait ses études au Goldsmiths College of Art. Il a travaillé comme designer indépendant avant d'entrer aux Beaverbrook Newspapers comme designer conseiller au "Daily Express," où il a mis en oeuvre l'utilisation de diagrammes et de tableaux pour illustrer les actualités quotidiennes sous forme graphique. En 1963 il est devenu Directeur artistique du "Sunday Times Magazine." Pendant quelque temps il est devenu Directeur de Design et Rédacteur en-Chef Adjoint du "Sunday Times." Toutefois, il est retourné au "Sunday Times Magazine" comme Directeur artistique et Rédacteur. Il a reçu de nombreux prix pour sa direction artistique, y compris les prix d'or et d'argent du D&AD.

Michael Rand studierte am Goldsmiths College of Art. Er arbeitete als freiberuflicher Designer und wurde dann beratender Designer der "Daily Express" innerhalb der Beaverbrook Zeitungsgruppe, wo er Pionierarbeiten mit Diagrammen und Tabellen zur grafischen Illustration der Nachrichten leistete. 1963 wurde er Kunstredakteur des "Sunday Times Magazine," danach für kurze Zeit Design Direktor und assoziierter Redakteur der "Sunday Times" und ging schließlich als Art Direktor und Chefredakteur zum "Sunday Times Magazine" zurück. Er hat viele Auszeichnungen für Art Direktion gewonnen, darunter die D&AD Silber- und Goldpreise.

M A X   S C H E L E R

Max Scheler was born in Cologne in 1928. After graduating from the University of Munich he went to Paris, where he worked as a magazine photographer for two years, and as junior member of "Magnum Photos" from 1954 to 1957. He then lived in Rome, covering political and cultural events for "Picture Post," "Paris Match" and "Münchner Illustrierte." He subsequently spent ten years as staff photographer of "Stern" magazine, and left to develop "Geo" with Gillhausen. Since 1981 he has been Managing Editor of "Merian" magazine and books.

Max Scheler est né à Cologne en 1928. Après avoir terminé ses études à l'Université de Munich, il est allé à Paris où il a travaillé comme photographe de magazine pendant deux ans et comme membre associé de "Magnum Photos" de 1954 à 1957. Il a ensuite vécu à Rome, comme reporter politique et culturel pour "Picture Post," "Paris Match" et "Münchner Illustrierte." Il a ensuite passé deux ans comme photographe officiel de "Stern" magazine, et l'a quitté pour développer "Geo" avec Gillhausen. Depuis 1981 il est Rédacteur en chef du magazine et des livres "Merian."

Max Scheler, geboren 1928 in Köln, ging nach Abschluß seines Studiums an der Universität München nach Paris, wo er zwei Jahre lang als Zeitschriften-Photograph und zwischen 1954 und 1957 als Junior-Mitglied von "Magnum Photos" arbeitete. Er zog nach Rom und berichtete über politische und kulturelle Ereignisse für "Picture Post," "Paris Match" und die "Münchner Illustrierte." Danach war er zehn Jahre lang Photograph beim "Stern," arbeitete zusammen mit Gillhausen am Aufbau der Zeitschrift "Geo" und ist seit 1981 Chefredakteur der "Merian" Zeitschriften und Bücher.

Gilvrie Misstear Designer · Maquettiste · Gestalter	Photographs for a series "The Taste of France" which appeared in "The Sunday Times Magazine." Mackerel from Dieppe for the feature on food from Normandy & Brittany by Adrian Bailey, March 1982.
Michael Rand Art Director · Directeur Artistique · Art Direktor	Photographies pour une série "The Taste of France" (Le goût de la France) qui a paru dans "The Sunday Times Magazine." Maquereaux de Dieppe pour un article sur la nourriture de Normandie et de Bretagne par Adrian Bailey, mars 1982.
Times Newspapers Limited Publisher · Editeur · Verleger	Photos für die Serie "The Taste of France" (Der Geschmack Frankreichs), erschienen in "The Sunday Times Magazine." Makrelen aus Dieppe, für den Artikel über Speisen aus der us der Normandie und der Bretagne von Adrian Bailey, März 1982.

Pumpkins, for the feature on food from the Languedoc by
Alan Davidson, April 1982.

Potirons, pour l'article sur la nourriture du Languedoc par
Alan Davidson, avril 1982.

Kürbisse, für den Artikel über Speisen aus der Languedoc von
Alan Davidson, April 1982.

Mike Lackersteen
Art Director · Directeur Artistique · Art Direktor

National Magazine Company
Publisher · Editeur · Verleger

Photograph for a feature "Grandmothers & Daughters" which appeared in "Good Housekeeping."

Photographie pour un article "Grandmothers & Daughters" (Grand-mères et filles) qui a paru dans "Good Housekeeping."

Photo für den Artikel "Grandmothers & Daughters" (Großmütter & Töchter), erschienen in "Good Housekeeping."

Photograph taken on location in Sweden for a travel feature which appeared in Scandinavia.

Photographie prise en extérieur en Suède pour un article de voyage qui a paru en Scandinavie.

Ein in Schweden aufgenommenes Photo für eine Reise-Reportage, erschienen in Skandinavien.

Dick De Moei
Art Director · Directeur Artistique · Art Direktor

Geillustreerde Pers
Publisher · Editeur · Verleger

2
2

Bob Giano
Art Director · Directeur Artistique · Art Direktor

John Loengard
Picture Editor · Directeur de Photographie · Bildredakteur

Time/Life Incorporated
Publisher · Editeur · Verleger

Photograph of school children in Toledo, Spain, where El Greco first worked at a nearby church, for a feature "To Ohio with Love" published in "Life" magazine, July 1982.

Photographie d'élèves à Tolède, Espagne, où El Greco a travaillé à ses débuts dans une église voisine, pour un article "To Ohio with Love" (A Ohio avec amour) publié dans "Life" magazine, juillet 1982.

Photo von Schulkindern in Toledo, Spanien, wo El Greco in seinen Anfängen in einer naheliegenden Kirche arbeitete; für den Artikel "To Ohio with Love" (Für Ohio mit lieben Grüßen), veröffentlicht in "Life," Juli 1982.

Photograph of Victor Lownes at his mansion "Stocks", to illustrate his obsession with fox-hunting for a feature published in "The Sunday Express Magazine", March 1983.

Photographie de Victor Lownes à son manoir "Stocks", pour montrer son obsession pour la chasse au renard, pour un article publié dans "The Sunday Express Magazine", mars 1983.

Photo von Victor Lownes in seinem Landhaus "Stocks", als Bekenntnis seiner Liebe für die Fuchsjagd, für einen Artikel in "The Sunday Express Magazine", veröffentlicht im März 1983.

Tom Reynolds
Art Director · Directeur Artistique · Art Direktor

Express Newspapers
Publisher · Editeur · Verleger

Photograph of Wigan Pier for the feature "Jack's Journeys'" by Ian Jack which appeared in the "The Sunday Times Magazine".

Photographie de la jetée de Wigan pour un article "Jack's Journeys" (les voyages de Jack) par Ian Jack qui a paru dans le "Sunday Times Magazine".

Photo des Wigan Pier für die Reportage "Jack's Journeys" (Jacks Reisen) von Ian Jack, erschienen in "The Sunday Times Magazine".

Pages 24, 25

Ian Denning
Designer · Maquettiste · Gestalter

John Tennant
Art Director · Directeur Artistique · Art Direktor

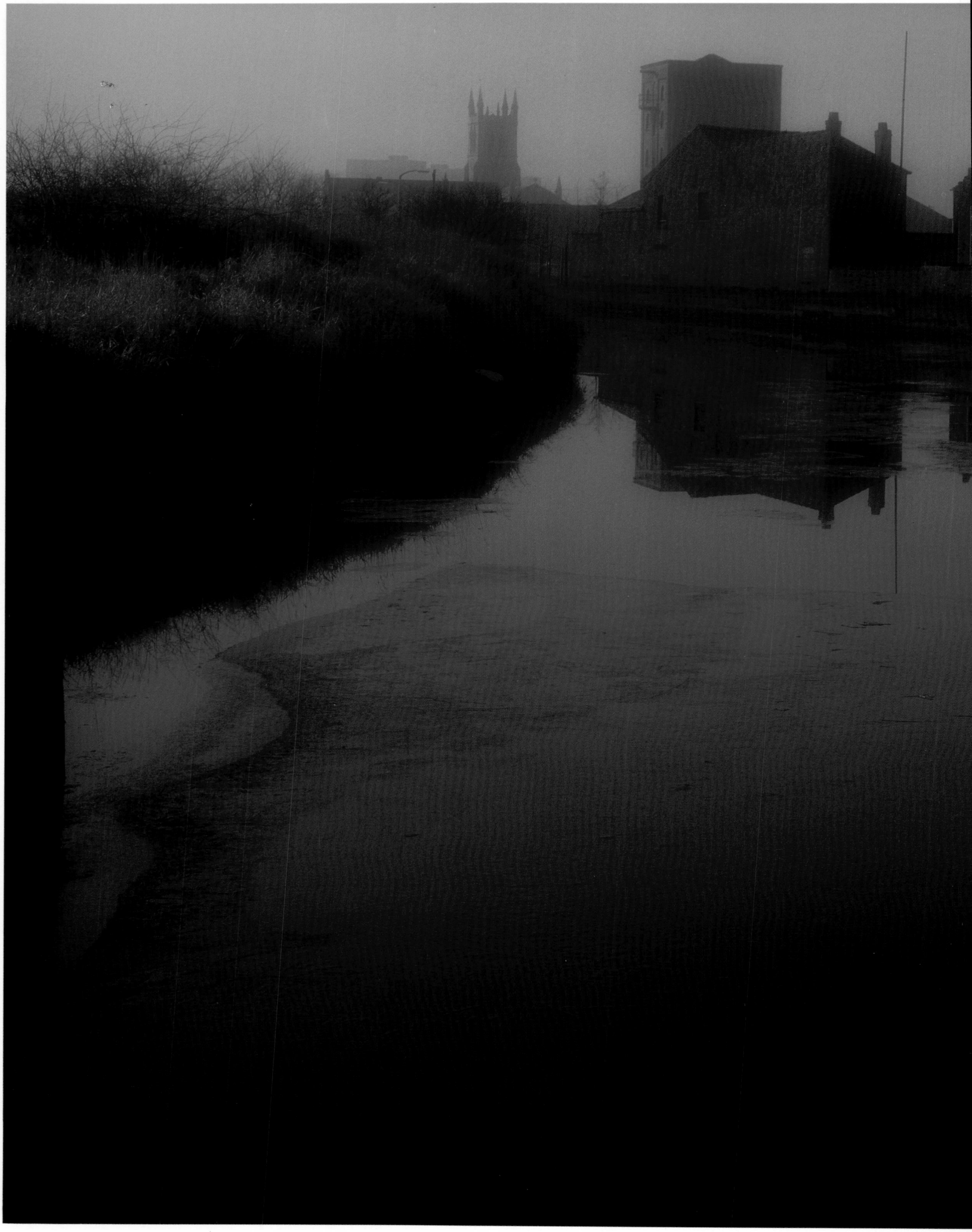

Pages 26 to 29

Wolfgang Behnken
Art Director · Directeur Artistique · Art Direktor

Gruner & Jahr AG & Co
Publisher · Editeur · Verleger

Photographs for the feature "Lustschlösser im Meer"
(Pleasure palaces in the sea) by Herbert Uniewski which
appeared in "Stern", September 1982.

Photographies pour l'article "Lustschlösser im Meer" (Palais
de plaisir dans la mer) par Herbert Uniewski qui a paru dans
"Stern", septembre 1982.

Photos für den Artikel "Lustschlösser im Meer" von Herbert
Uniewski, erschienen im "Stern", September 1982.

Detlef Schlottmann Designer · Maquettiste · Gestalter	Photograph for a feature "Eishockey in Russland" (Ice-hockey in Russia) which appeared in "Stern", May 1983.
Rolf Gillhausen Art Director · Directeur Artistique · Art Direktor	Photographie pour un article "Eishockey in Russland" (Hockey sur glace en Russie) qui a paru dans "Stern", mai 1983.
Gruner & Jahr AG & Co Publisher · Editeur · Verleger	Photo für den Artikel "Eishockey in Russland", erschienen im "Stern", Mai 1983.

3 ——
1 ——

Photograph for a feature "The Ice Man Cometh", published in
"The Sunday Times Magazine" in December 1982.

Photographie pour un article "The Ice Man Cometh" (L'Homme
de glace arrive) publié dans "The Sunday Times Magazine" en
décembre 1982.

Photo für den Artikel "The Ice Man Cometh" (Der Eis-Mann
kommt), veröffentlicht in "The Sunday Times Magazine" im
Dezember 1982.

Graeme Murdoch
Art Director · Directeur Artistique · Art Direktor

Colin Jacobson
Picture Editor · Directeur de Photographie · Bildredakteur

The Observer Magazine
Publisher · Editeur · Verleger

Photograph taken on board the QE2 on the way to the Falkland war with the Welsh Guards for a feature "The Sergeant Major's War" by Alan Road, which appeared in "The Observer Magazine," October 1982.

Photographie prise à bord du QE2 en route pour la guerre des Falklands avec les Welsh Guards pour un article "The Sergeant Major's War" (La Guerre de l'Adjudant chef) par Alan Road, qui a paru dans "The Observer Magazine," octobre 1982.

Photo, aufgenommen an Bord der QE2 auf dem Weg zu den Falkland Inseln mit den Welsh Guards, für die Reportage "The Sergeant Major's War" (Der Feldwebel-Krieg) von Alan Road, erschienen in "The Observer Magazine," Oktober 1982.

Photograph of the 42 Commando going ashore at Port San Carlos in the Falklands for a feature "The Longest Year" in "The Sunday Times Magazine," April 1982.

Photographie du 42 Commando débarquant à Port San Carlos aux Falklands pour un article "The Longest Year" (L'année la plus longue) dans "The Sunday Times Magazine," avril 1982.

Photo des 42 Commandos während der Landung in Port San Carlos in den Falkland Inseln, für die Reportage "The Longest Year" (Das längste Jahr), in "The Sunday Times Magazine," April 1982.

John Tennant
Designer · Maquettiste · Gestalter

Michael Rand
Art Director · Directeur Artistique · Art Direktor

Times Newspapers Limited
Publisher · Editeur · Verleger

3
4

Pages 34 to 37

Franz Epping
Designer · Maquettiste · Gestalter

Rolf Gillhausen
Art Director · Directeur Artistique · Art Direktor

Gruner & Jahr AG & Co
Publisher · Editeur · Verleger

Photographs for a feature "Begegnungen zwischen Mensch und Tier" (Encounters between man and beast) published in "Stern", 1982.

Photographies pour un article "Begegnungen zwischen Mensch und Tier" (Rencontres entre homme et bête) publié dans "Stern", 1982.

Photos für den Artikel "Begegnungen zwischen Mensch und Tier," veröffentlicht im "Stern", 1982.

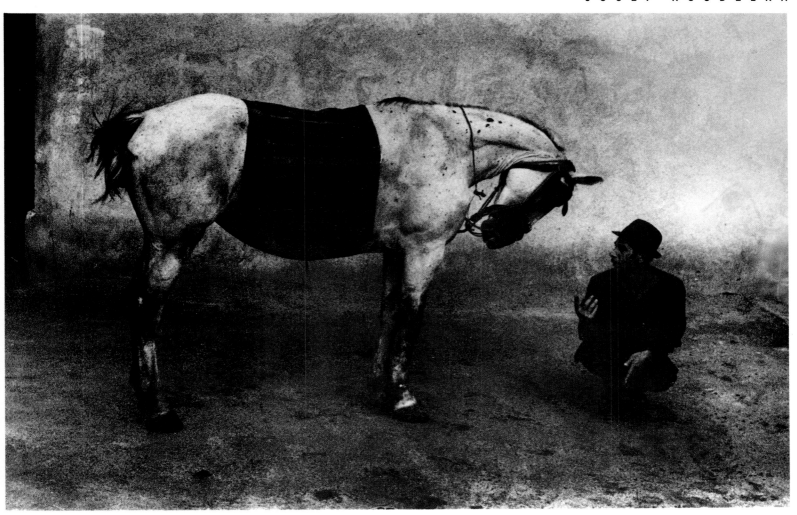

3
6

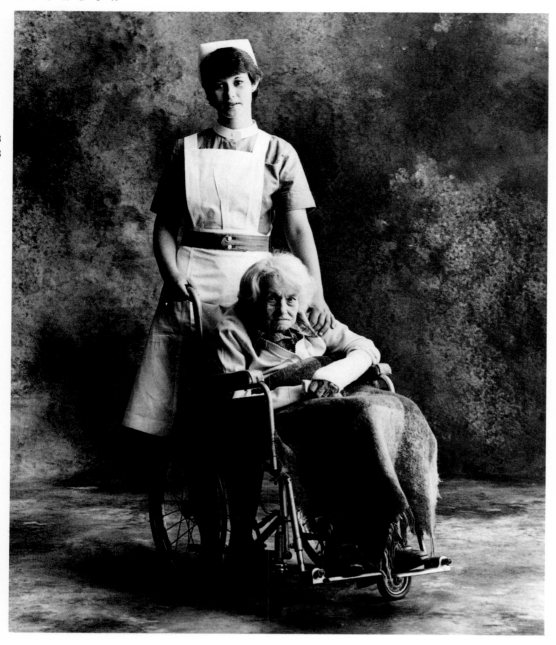

Pages 38 to 43

Gerald Peak
Designer · Maquettiste · Gestalter

Molly Godet
Art Director · Directeur Artistique · Art Direktor

McCormick Intermarco·Farner Limited
Advertising Agency · Agence de Publicité · Werbeagentur

Photographs of hospital workers taken while on duty at St. Mary Abbot's, Kensington, for a calendar which appeared in September 1982.

Photographies du personnel d'hôpital prises en temp de service à l'hôpital St. Mary Abbot's à Kensington, pour un calendrier qui a paru en septembre 1982.

Photos von Krankenhaus·Personal während der Arbeit im St. Mary Abbot's Krankenhaus in Kensington, für einen Kalender, erschienen im September 1982.

SNOWDON

4
1

4
2

Pages 44 to 47

Herbert Suhr
Designer · Maquettiste · Gestalter

Rolf Gillhausen
Art Director · Directeur Artistique · Art Direktor

Gruner & Jahr AG & Co
Publisher · Editeur · Verleger

Photographs for the feature "Deutschland im März" (Germany in March) published in "Stern", 1982.
Cut price offers.

Photographies pour l'article "Deutschland im März" (L'Allemagne en marche) publié dans "Stern", 1982.
Occasions.

Photos für den Artikel "Deutschland im März," veröffentlicht im "Stern," 1982.
Billigangebote.

Pedestrian underpass, invalid playing the accordion, passers-
by dancing spontaneously.

Passage souterrain pour piétons, infirme jouant de
l'accordéon, passants dansant spontanément.

Fußgängerunterführung, beinamputierter spielt Akkordeon,
Passanten tanzen spontan.

4
6

Barbed wire at the nuclear power station Brokdorf.

Fil de fer barbelé à la centrale nucléaire de Brokdorf.

Stacheldraht am Atommeiler Brokdorf.

An artist in front of the National Gallery in West Berlin,
painting a landscape superimposed by the swastika.

Artiste devant la Galerie Nationale à Berlin ouest, peignant un
paysage avec en surempression la croix gammée.

Vor der Westberliner Nationalgalerie malt ein Künstler eine
Landschaft, über der das Hakenkreuz liegt.

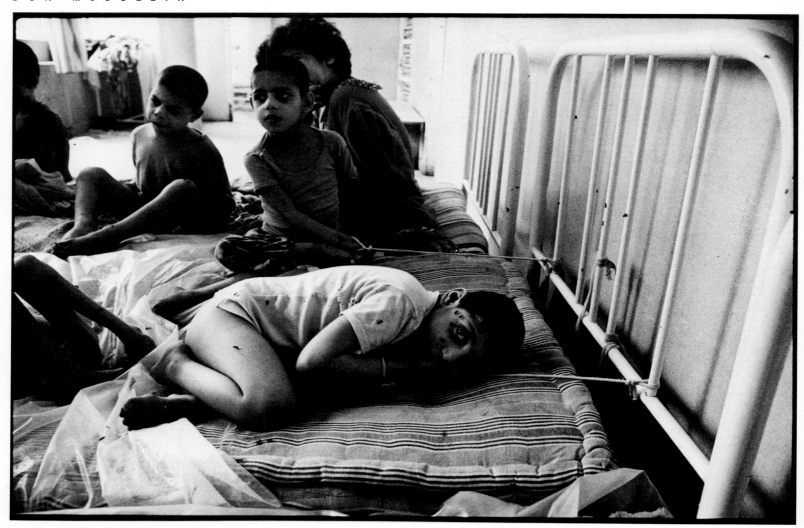

Photograph of mentally retarded children tied to their beds in a mental hospital during the siege of Beirut, for a feature on Beirut in "The Sunday Times Magazine," August 1982.

Photographie d'enfants handicapés mentaux attachés à leur lit dans un hôpital psychiatrique pendant le siège de Beyrouth, pour un article sur Beyrouth dans "The Sunday Times Magazine," août 1982.

Photo von geistig behinderten Kindern, festgebunden an ihre Betten in einem Krankenhaus während der Belagerung Beiruts, für einen Artikel über Beirut in "The Sunday Times Magazine," August 1982.

Photograph of troops dragging away the corpse of a dead
guerilla in San Salvador, for a feature on El Salvador in "The
Sunday Times Magazine," June 1982.

Photographie de troupes emmenant le corps d'un guerilla
mort au San Salvador, pour un article sur El Salvador dans
"The Sunday Times Magazine," juin 1982.

Photo von Truppen bei der Bergung eines toten Guerilla in San
Salvador, für einen Artikel über El Salvador in "The Sunday
Times Magazine," Juni 1982.

5
0

Pages 50 to 56

Willy Fleckhaus
Art Director · Directeur Artistique · Art Direktor

Frankfurter Allgemeine Zeitung GmbH
Publisher · Editeur · Verleger

A series of photographs from a feature, "Wo es um die Wurst geht: Hausschlachten," (When it comes to sausages, slaughter at home).
The pig is stunned before the kill.

Série de photographies pour un article "Wo es um die Wurst geht: Hausschlachten" (Quand il s'agit de saucisses, il faut tuer chez soi).
Le porc est assommé avant d'être tué.

Eine Reihe von Photos für den Artikel "Wo es um die Wurst geht: Hausschlachten."
Kurz vor dem Schuß wird die Sau betäubt.

5

1

A drink in celebration.

Un pot pour célébrer.

Ein Schnaps zur Feier des Tages.

The bristles are shaved.

Les poils sont rasés.

Die Borsten werden wegrasiert.

The carcass on display outside the farmhouse.

La carcasse exposée à la porte de la ferme.

Der Schlachtkörper aufgehängt vor dem Hof.

Boiling in the pot.

Cuisson en marmite.

Würste im kochenden Wasserkessel.

Page 55 The first sausages are ready.

Les premières saucisses sont prêtes.

Die ersten Würste sind fertig.

Sausages hanging up to dry.

Les saucisses sont pendues pour sécher.

Die Würste aufgereiht zum Trocknen.

Photograph for a feature "A Walk Among the Vines" by Nigel Buxton, showing the author checking his map at dawn in the Sancerre wine region of France; published in "The Telegraph Sunday Magazine."

Photographie pour un article "A Walk Among the Vines" (Promenade dans les vignes) par Nigel Buxton, montrant l'auteur en train de vérifier sa carte à l'aube dans la région du Sancerre en France, publiée dans "The Telegraph Sunday Magazine."

Photo für den Artikel "A Walk Among the Vines" (Ein Spaziergang zwischen den Weinreben) von Nigel Buxton, mit dem Autor, der in der Morgendämmerung seine Karte der Sancerre Weinregion in Frankreich überprüft; veröffentlicht in "The Telegraph Sunday Magazine."

Ian Bradshaw
Picture Editor · Directeur de Photographie · Bildredakteur

The Sunday Telegraph Limited
Publisher · Editeur · Verleger

Simon Esterson
Designer · Maquettiste · Gestalter

The Architectural Press
Publisher · Editeur · Verleger

Portrait of Philip Johnson in his office in New York, for a feature by Colin Amery, "Johnson's Cookie Cutter Modern"; The Architects' Journal, February 1983.

Portrait de Philip Johnson dans son bureau à New York, pour un article par Colin Amery, "Johnson's Cookie Cutter Modern" (Le style moderne de Johnson); The Architects' Journal, février 1983.

Porträt von Philip Johnson in seinem Büro in New York, für einen Artikel von Colin Amery, "Johnson's Cookie Cutter Modern"; (Johnsons Plätzchenform Moderne;) "The Architects' Journal," Februar 1983.

Photograph of the Bristol Rock & Roll Appreciation Society's re-union at Pontin's Holiday Camp, published in "The Sunday Times Magazine" in October 1982.

Photographie d'une réunion anniversaire de la Société d'Appréciation du Rock & Roll de Bristol au camp de vacances Pontins, publiée dans "The Sunday Times Magazine" en octobre 1982.

Photo der Bristol Rock 'n' Roll Würdigungs-Gesellschaft bei ihrem Treffen im Pontins Ferien-Camp, veröffentlicht in "The Sunday Times Magazine" im Oktober 1982.

John Tennant
Art Director · Directeur Artistique · Art Direktor

Pages 60, 61

Dietmar Schulze
Designer · Maquettiste · Gestalter

Rolf Gillhausen
Art Director · Directeur Artistique · Art Direktor

Gruner & Jahr AG & Co
Publisher · Editeur · Verleger

Photographs for a feature "Spreewald" (Spree-Forest) which appeared in "Stern" in 1982.

Photographies pour un article "Spreewald" (La Forêt de Spree) qui a paru dans "Stern" 1982.

Photos für den Artikel "Spreewald," erschienen im "Stern," 1982.

Photograph for the article "Review of Operations: United Kingdom" which appeared in the "Annual Report 1982" in June 1982.

Photographie pour l'article "Review of Operations: United Kingdom" (Revue des opérations: Royaume-Uni) qui a paru dans le "Annual Report 1982" en juin 1982.

Photo für den Artikel "Review of Operations: United Kingdom" (Rückblick auf Vorgänge: das Vereinigte Königreich), erschienen in "Annual Report 1982", Juni 1982.

Pages 62, 63

John Tennant
Designer · Maquettiste · Gestalter

Michael Rand
Art Director · Directeur Artistique · Art Direktor

News Corporation
Publisher · Editeur · Verleger

Joanne Dale
Art Director · Directeur Artistique · Art Direktor

The Observer Magazine
Publisher · Editeur · Verleger

Photograph taken in Park Lane Hotel for a feature "Thoroughly Modern Millie," which appeared in "The Observer Magazine" in December 1982.

Photographie prise dans le Park Lane Hotel pour un article "Thoroughly Modern Millie" (Millie tout à fait moderne) qui a paru dans "The Observer Magazine" en décembre 1982.

Photo, aufgenommen im Park Lane Hotel, für den Artikel "Thoroughly Modern Millie" (Die ausgesprochen moderne Millie), erschienen in "The Observer Magazine," Dezember 1982.

Photographs for the feature "Freiheit Heilt" (Freedom heals)
on mental institutions in Italy, which appeared in "Stern" in
1982.

Photographies pour l'article "Freiheit Heilt" (La liberté guérit)
sur les institutions psychiatriques en Italie, qui a paru dans
"Stern" en 1982.

Photos für den Artikel "Freiheit Heilt" über Heilanstalten in
Italien, erschienen im "Stern," 1982.

Pages 65 to 73

Jan Görlich
Designer · Maquettiste · Gestalter

Rolf Gillhausen
Art Director · Directeur Artistique · Art Direktor

Gruner & Jahr AG & Co
Publisher · Editeur · Verleger

6
8

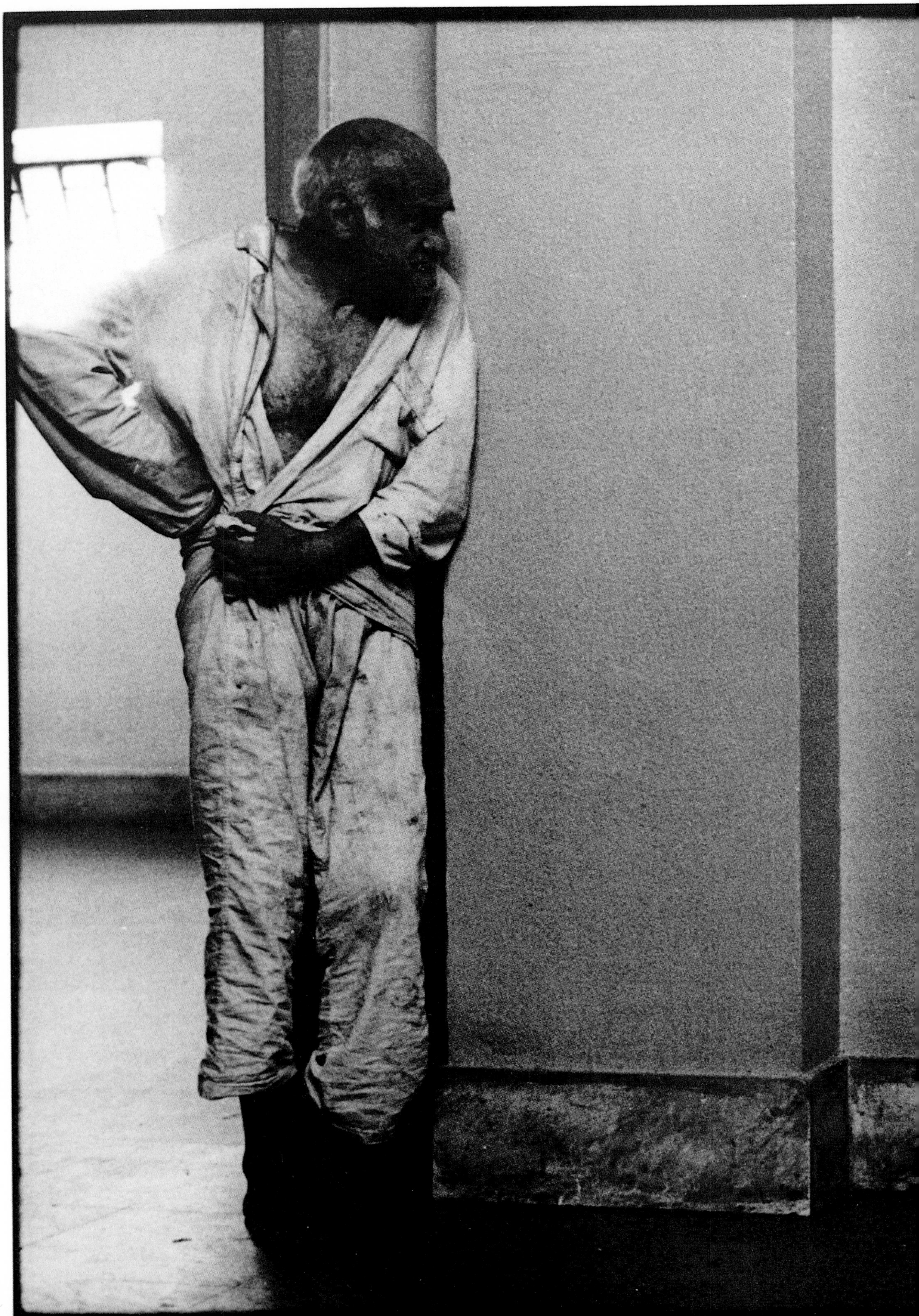

7
2

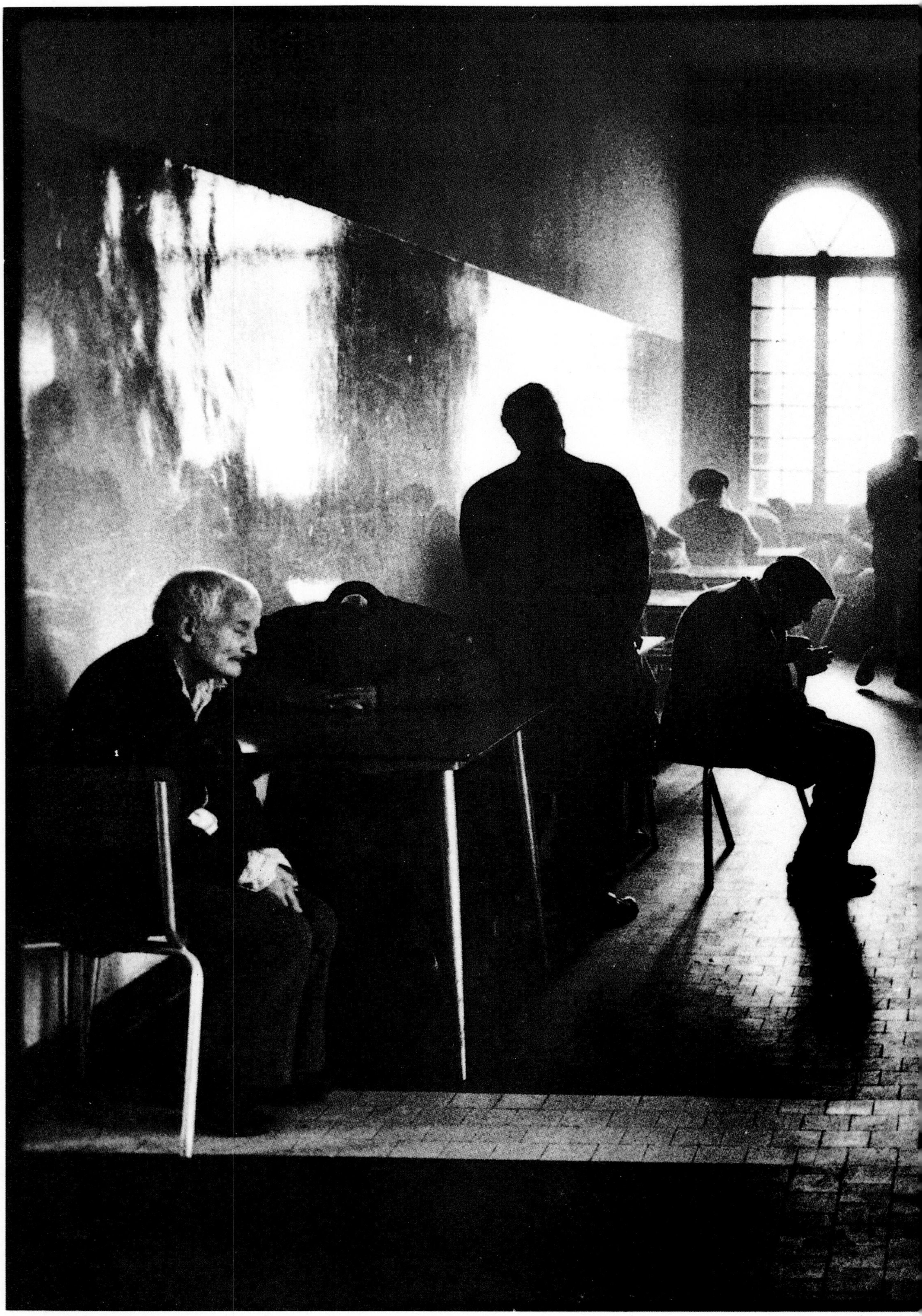

K.E.O. Smith
Art Director · Directeur Artistique · Art Direktor

Times Newspapers Limited
Publisher · Editeur · Verleger

Photograph of Ian Paisley taken at an Orange Lodge meeting in Crumlin, near Belfast, for a feature which appeared in "The Times."

Photographie d'Ian Paisley prise à un meeting du Orange Lodge à Crumlin, près de Belfast, pour un article paru dans "The Times."

Photo von Ian Paisley, aufgenommen bei einer Versammlung der Orange Lodge in Crumlin, in der Nähe von Belfast, für eine Reportage erschienen in "The Times."

Page 75

David Driver
Designer · Maquettiste · Gestalter

Michael Young
Picture Editor · Directeur de Photographie · Bildredakteur

Times Newspapers Limited
Publisher · Editeur · Verleger

Portrait of Dirk Bogarde for a profile feature by Nicholas Wapshott which appeared in "The Times."

Portrait de Dirk Bogarde pour un article biographique par Nicholas Wapshott qui a paru dans "The Times."

Porträt von Dirk Bogarde für einen biografischen Artikel von Nicholas Wapshott, erschienen in "The Times."

7
6

David Driver
Designer · Maquettiste · Gestalter

Portrait of Malcolm Muggeridge which appeared in "The Times",
March 1983.

Michael Young
Picture Editor · Directeur de Photographie · Bildredakteur

Portrait de Malcolm Muggeridge qui a paru dans "The Times",
mars 1983,

Times Newspapers Limited
Publisher · Editeur · Verleger

Porträt von Malcolm Muggeridge, erschienen in "The Times",
März 1983.

Portrait of Sir William Walton which appeared in "The Times,"
March 1983.

David Driver
Designer · Maquettiste · Gestalter

Portrait de Sir William Walton qui a paru dans "The Times,"
mars 1983.

Keith Smith
Picture Editor · Directeur de Photographie · Bildredakteur

Porträt von Sir William Walton, erschienen in "The Times,"
März 1983.

Times Newspapers Limited
Publisher · Editeur · Verleger

David Driver
Designer · Maquettiste · Gestalter

Portrait of Samuel Beckett which was used for an Arts Page Feature in "The Times."

Michael Young
Picture Editor · Directeur de Photographie · Bildredakteur

Portrait de Samuel Beckett utilisé pour un article de la page des Arts dans "The Times."

Times Newspapers Limited
Publisher · Editeur · Verleger

Porträt von Samuel Beckett, eingesetzt für einen Artikel in den Kunstseiten in "The Times."

Portrait of Sir Roy Strong for a feature by himself on the
Victoria and Albert Museum which appeared in "The Times",
March 1983.

Portrait de Sir Roy Strong pour un article par lui-même sur le
Victoria and Albert Museum, qui a paru dans "The Times",
mars 1983.

Porträt von Sir Roy Strong für einen von ihm verfaßten Artikel
über das Victoria und Albert Museum, erschienen in "The
Times", März 1983.

David Driver
Designer · Maquettiste · Gestalter

Michael Young
Picture Editor · Directeur de Photographie · Bildredakteur

Times Newspapers Limited.
Publisher · Editeur · Verleger

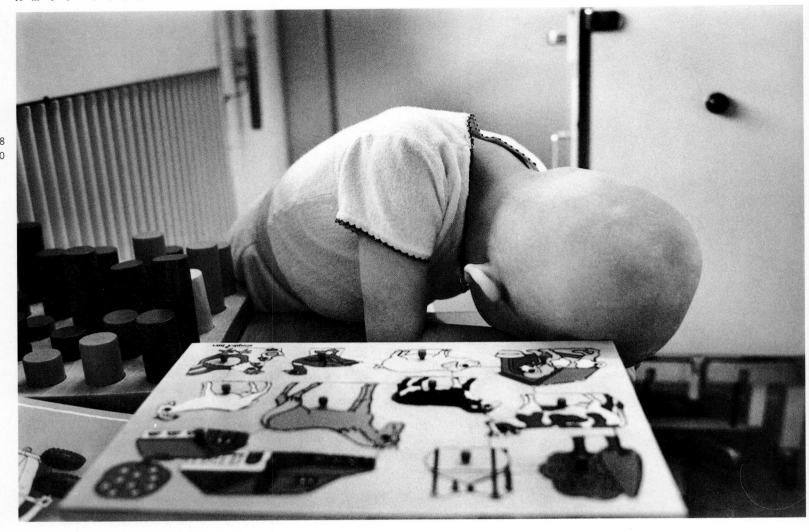

Pages 80 to 83   Photographs for a feature "Station Peiper" (Peiper Ward) by
Inga Thomsen on a clinic for children which appeared in
Max Lengwenus   "Stern," March 1982.
Designer · Maquettiste · Gestalter

Photographies pour un article "Station Peiper" (Salle Peiper)
Franz Kliebhan   par Inga Thomsen sur une clinique pour enfants qui a paru
Art Director · Directeur Artistique · Art Direktor   dans "Stern" mars 1982.

Gruner & Jahr AG & Co   Photos für den Artikel "Station Peiper" von Inga Thomsen über
Publisher · Editeur · Verleger   eine Kinder-Klinik, erschienen im "Stern," März 1982.

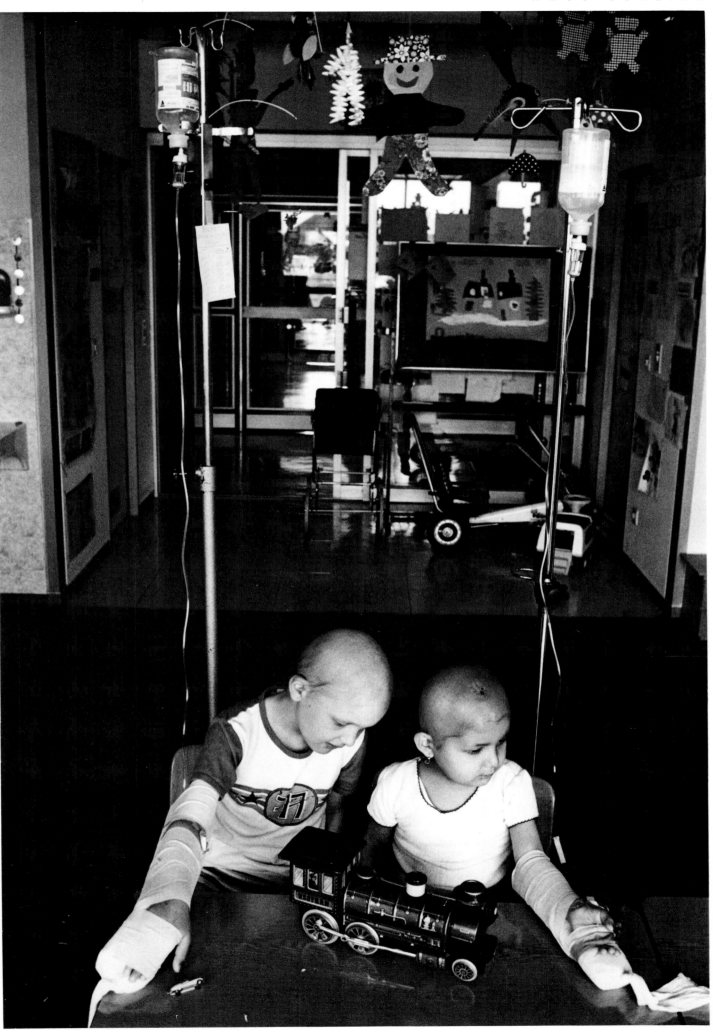

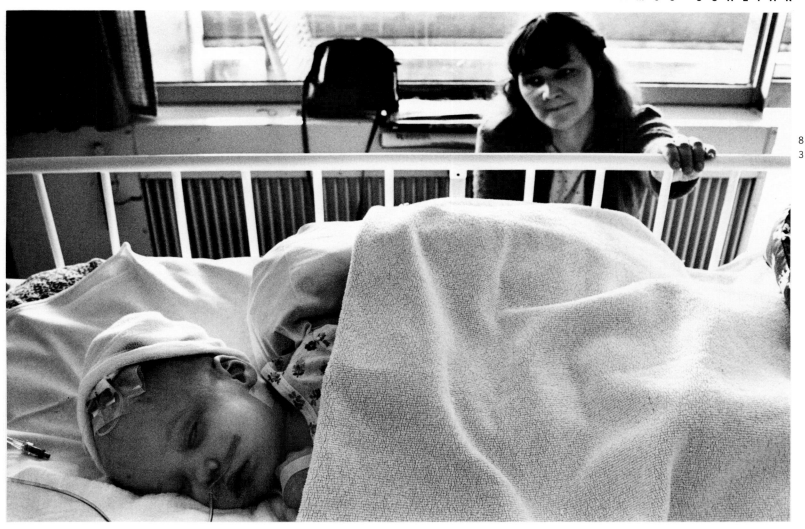

Photograph taken in the Reading Room of The London Library, St. James Square, to illustrate a feature by Sebastian Cody, "London Library", which appeared in "The Tatler", June 1983.

Photographie prise dans la Salle de Lecture de la London Library, St. James's Square, pour illustrer un article de Sebastian Cody, "London Library", qui a paru dans "The Tatler" en juin 1983.

Photo, aufgenommen im Lesesaal der Londoner Bibliothek in St. James Square, für eine Reportage von Sebastian Cody, "London Library", erschienen in "The Tatler", Juni 1983.

Pages 84, 85

Michael Roberts
Art Director · Directeur Artistique · Art Direktor

Condé Nast Publications Ltd
Publisher · Editeur · Verleger

8
6

K.E.O Smith
Art Director · Directeur Artistique · Art Direktor

Times Newspapers Limited
Publisher · Editeur · Verleger

Photograph of Malik Atta tent-pegging on Rotten Row at dawn, for a feature by Brian Harris on the Royal Tournament in "The Times."

Photographie de Malik Atta fixant sa tente à l'aube dans Rotten Row pour un article de Brian Harris sur le Royal Tournament dans "The Times."

Photo von Malik Atta beim Zeltaufstellen in der Morgen-dämmerung in Rotten Row, für eine Reportage von Brian Harris über das Royal Tournament in "The Times."

"Sports Photo of the Year" taken at the Commonwealth Games in Brisbane, which appeared in "The Sunday Times," February 1983.

"Sports Photo of the Year" (La Photo-Sport de l'année) prise aux Commonwealth Games à Brisbane, qui a paru dans "The Sunday Times," février 1983.

"Sports Photo of the Year" (Das Sport-Photo des Jahres), aufgenommen während der Commonwealth-Spiele in Brisbane und erschienen in "The Sunday Times," Februar 1983.

Times Newspapers Limited
Publisher · Editeur · Verleger

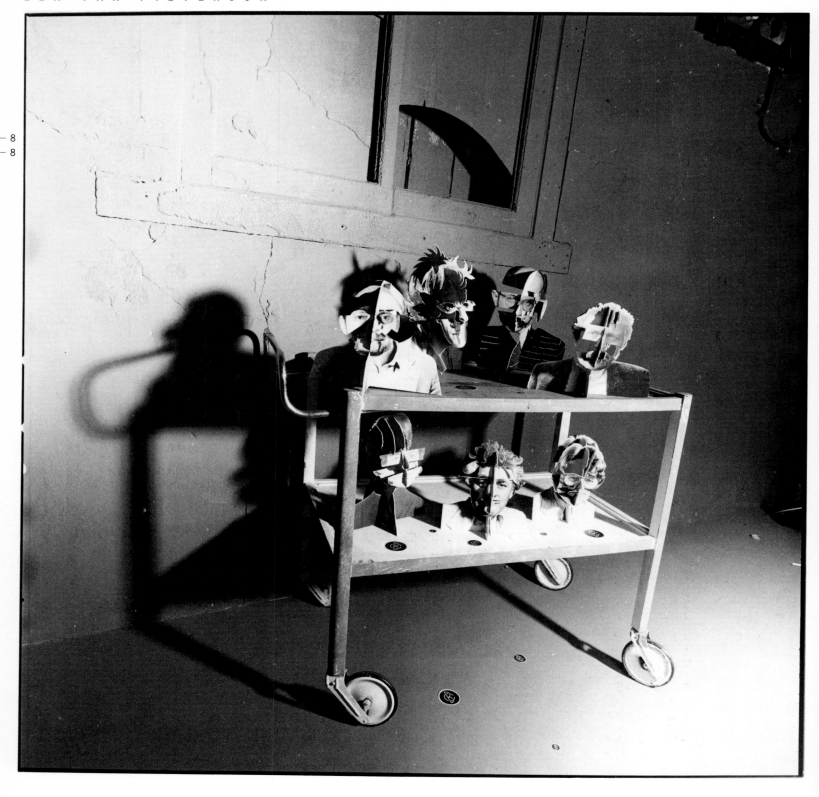

8
8

Berry Van Gerven
Designer · Maquettiste · Gestalter

Gert Dumbar
Art Director · Directeur Artistique · Art Direktor

Photograph of the "portraits" of the chairman and members of
the jury of the ninth European Illustration, published in the
annual, October 1982.

Photographie des "portraits" du président et membres du jury
du neuvième European Illustration, publiée dans l'annuaire,
octobre 1982.

Photo der "Porträts" des Vorsitzenden und der Jury-Mitglieder
des neunten European Illustration, veröffentlicht im Jahrbuch,
Oktober 1982.

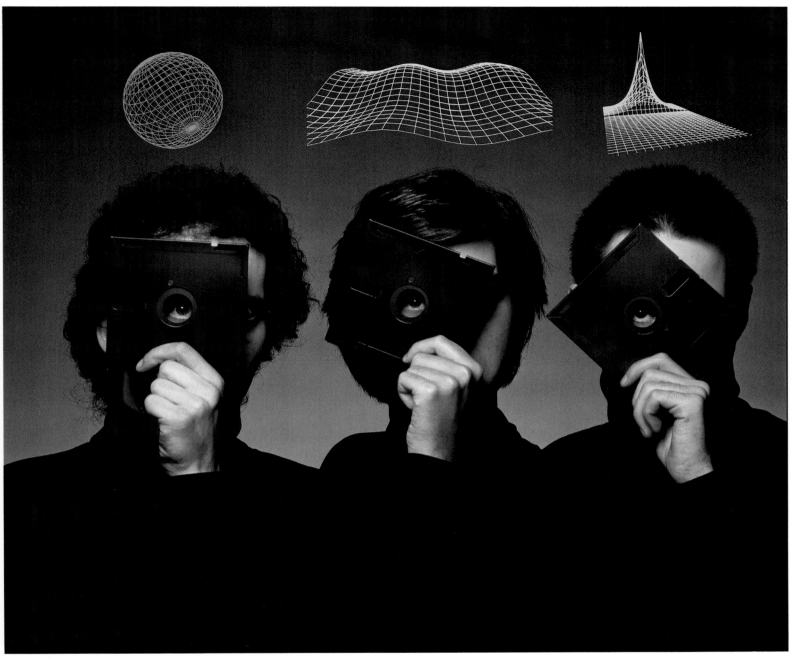

Photograph for a feature "Secrets of the Software Pirates" by Lee Gomes, published in "Esquire" in January 1982.

Photographie pour un article "Secrets of the Software Pirates" (Les secrets des pirates du software) par Lee Gomes, publié dans "Esquire" en janvier 1982.

Photo für den Artikel "Die Geheimnisse der Software Piraten" von Lee Gomes, veröffentlicht in "Esquire" im Januar 1982.

Jennifer Crandall
Picture Editor · Directeur de Photographie · Bildredakteur

Esquire Publishing Inc.
Publisher · Editeur · Verleger

Pages 90 to 98

Wolfgang Behnken/Rolf Gillhausen
Art Directors · Directeurs Artistiques · Art Direktoren

Gruner & Jahr AG & Co
Publisher · Editeur · Verleger

Photographs for a feature "Amerika auf dem roten Sofa"
(America on the Red Couch) by Eva Windmoeller which
appeared in "Stern," May 1983.
Bill Bradford, an American driver, with Japanese car imports
in Los Angeles.

Photographies pour un article "Amerika auf dem roten Sofa"
(L'Amérique sur le sofa rouge) par Eva Windmoeller qui a paru
dans "Stern," mai 1983.
Bill Bradford, conducteur américain, avec voitures importées
du Japon à Los Angeles.

Photos für die Reportage "Amerika auf dem roten Sofa" von
Eva Windmoeller, erschienen im "Stern," Mai 1983.
Bill Bradford, ein amerikanischer Autofahrer, mit Importwagen
aus Japan in Los Angeles.

The fire department in Great Jones Street, New York.

Les sapeurs pompiers de Great Jones Street, New York.

Die Feuerwehr in Great Jones Street, New York.

Hugh Hefner and bunnies at his mansion in Beverly Hills,
Hollywood, California.

Hugh Hefner et hôtesses dans son manoir de Beverly Hills,
Hollywood, Californie.

Hugh Hefner und Häschen in seinem Haus in Beverly Hills,
Hollywood, Kalifornien.

Page 93   Michael Weeks, director of space transportation at NASA,
Cape Canaveral, Florida.

Michael Weeks, directeur de transport dans l'espace au NASA,
Cap Canaveral, Floride.

Michael Weeks, Direktor des Raumfahrt-Programms der
NASA, Cape Canaveral, Florida.

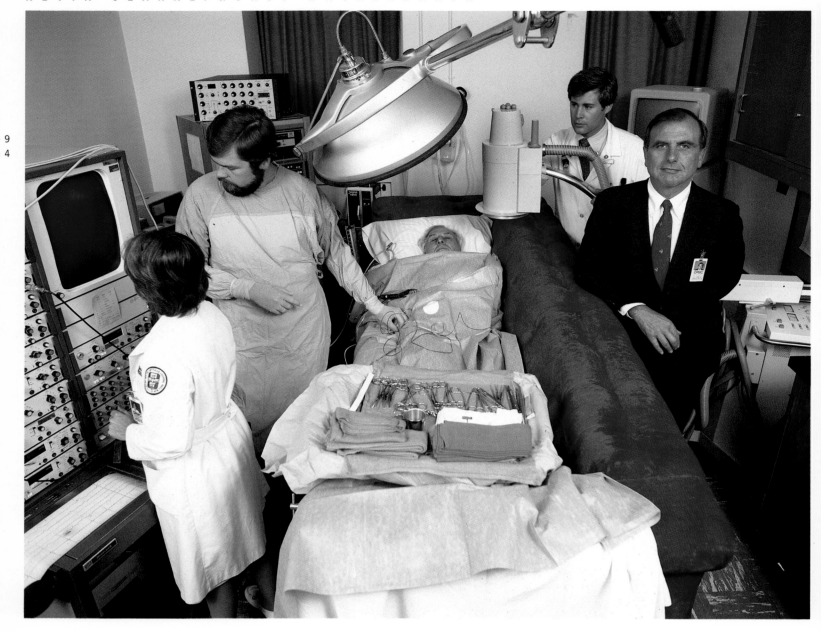

Cardiologists and the Head of Administration at the Columbia
Presbyterian Hospital, New York.

Cardiologues et le Chef d'Administration au Columbia
Presbyterian Hospital, New York.

Kardiologen und der Verwaltungschef im Columbia
Presbyterian Hospital, New York.

James Porter of the New York City Police, in the 17th precinct
detective unit, New York.

James Porter de la Police de New York City, de la section de
sûreté de la 17e circonscription, New York.

James Porter, Mitglied der New York City Police, im 17. Polizei-
Revier in New York.

Elmer Greene with a bear in Beartown Valley, Vermont.   Pages 96, 97

Elmer Greene avec un ours dans Beartown Valley, Vermont.

Elmer Greene mit einem Bär in Beartown Valley, Vermont.

Dr Nathan Kline, a psychiatrist in New York.

Dr Nathan Kline, psychiatre à New York.

Dr. Nathan Kline, ein Psychiater in New York.

A series of photographs for a fashion feature by Vincent Boucher in "Esquire," March 1983.

Série de photographies pour un article sur la mode par Vincent Boucher dans "Esquire," mars 1983.

Eine Reihe von Photos für einen Mode-Bericht von Vincent Boucher in "Esquire," März 1983.

Pages 99 to 105

Jennifer Crandall
Picture Editor · Directeur de Photographie · Bildredakteur

Robert Priest/April Silver
Art Directors · Directeurs Artistiques · Art Direktoren

Esquire Publishing Inc.
Publisher · Editeur · Verleger

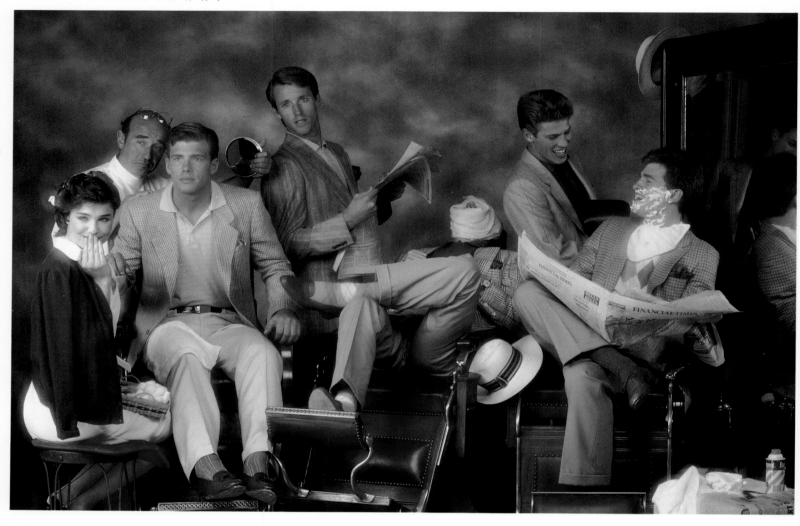

1
0
6

Franz Epping
Designer · Maquettiste · Gestalter

Photograph for a feature on housing problems which appeared in "Stern" in 1982.

Wolfgang Behnken
Art Director · Directeur Artistique · Art Direktor

Photographie pour un article sur les problèmes de logement qui a paru dans "Stern" en 1982.

Gruner & Jahr AG & Co
Publisher · Editeur · Verleger

Photo für einen Artikel über die Wohnungsnot, erschienen im "Stern," 1982.

Photograph for a feature "Nie Wieder Krieger" (Never again warriors) by Tepilit Ole Saitoti, showing the Masai in Kenya drinking the blood of a cow, published in 'Stern', April 1982.

Photographie pour un reportage "Nie Wieder Krieger" (Plus jamais de Combattants) par Tepilit Ole Saitoti, montrant les Masai au Kenya buvant du sang de vache, publiée dans 'Stern', avril 1982.

Photo für die Reportage "Nie wieder Krieger" von Tepilit Ole Saitoti, das die Masai in Kenia beim Trinken des Blutes einer Kuh zeigt. Veröffentlicht im 'Stern', April 1982.

Gruner & Jahr AG & Co
Publisher · Editeur · Verleger

Pages 108 to 113

Dietmar Meyer
Designer · Maquettiste · Gestalter

Victor Schuller
Editor · Editeur · Redakteur

Gruner & Jahr AG & Co
Publisher · Editeur · Verleger

Wibke Bruhns
Writer · Auteur · Autor

Photographs from the book "Mein Jerusalem" (My Jerusalem).
Fight for the last drop of sacred water.

Photographies du livres "Mein Jerusalem" (Ma Jerusalem)
Bagarre pour la dernière goutte d'eau sacrée.

Photos aus dem Buch "Mein Jerusalem."
Kampf um den letzten geweihten Wassertropfen.

American pilgrim at the Via Dolorosa on Good Friday.

Pèlerin américain à la Via Dolorosa le vendredi saint.

Amerikanischer Pilger am Karfreitag auf der Via Dolorosa.

Midday Friday at the central bus station in West Jerusalem.

Vendredi à midi à la station centrale d'autobus à Jerusalem ouest.

Freitagmittag auf dem zentralen Bus-Bahnhof in West-Jerusalem.

Muslim trader/Jewish beggar.

Commerçant musulman/mendiant juif.

Moslemischer Händler/jüdischer Bettler.

Arab traders at the sheep market on Friday morning.   Pages 112, 113

Commerçants arabes au marché aux moutons un vendredi
matin.

Arabische Händler auf dem Schafmarkt am Freitagmorgen.

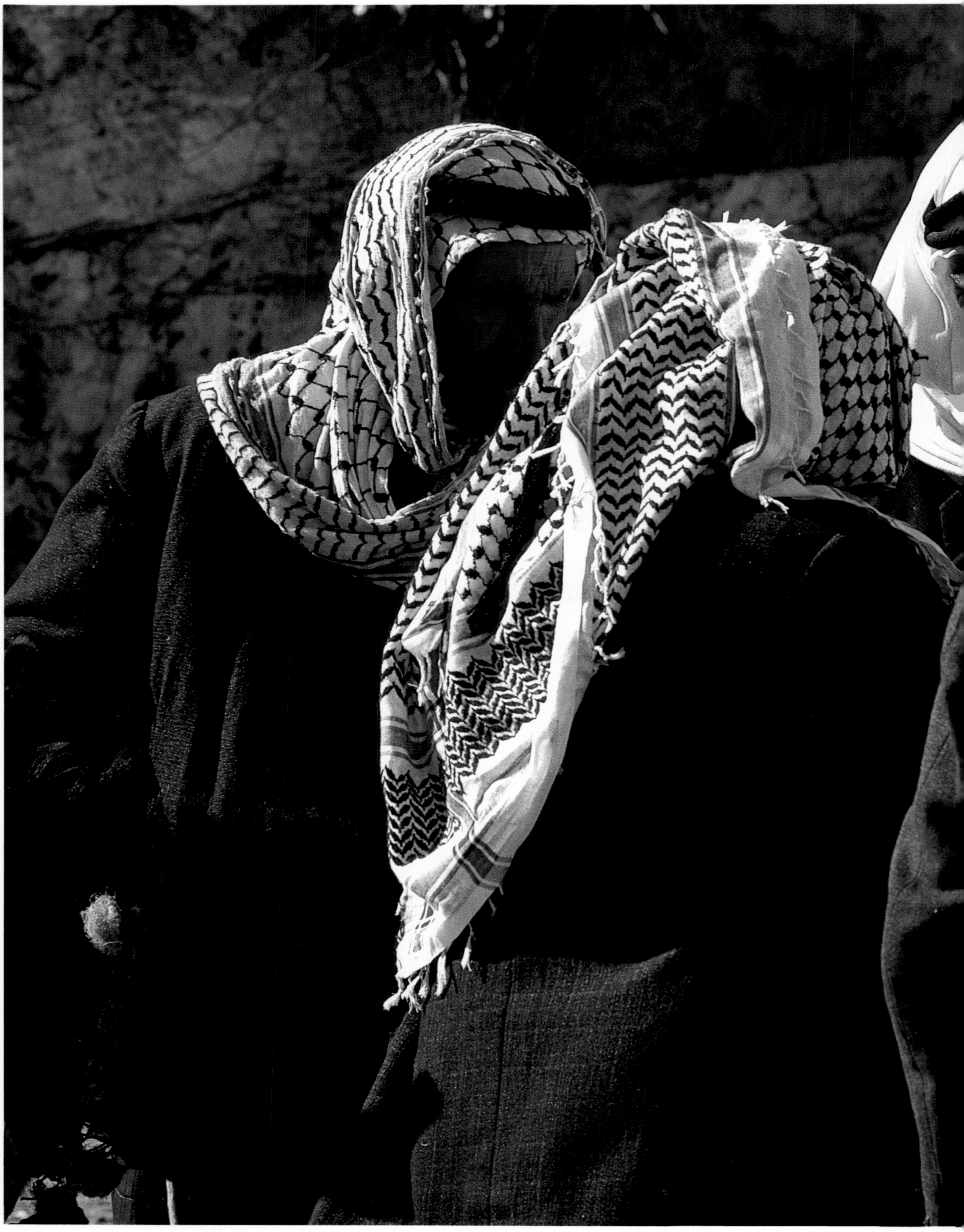

Pages 116 to 122   Photographs from the book "Wales: The First Place."

Neil Clitheroe   Photographies du livre "Wales: The First Place" (Pays de
Designer · Maquettiste · Gestalter   Galles: premier lieu).

Aurum Press   Photos aus dem Buch "Wales: The First Place." (Wales: Die
Publisher · Editeur · Verleger   Ursprungsstätte).

Jan Morris
Writer · Auteur · Autor

1
1
8

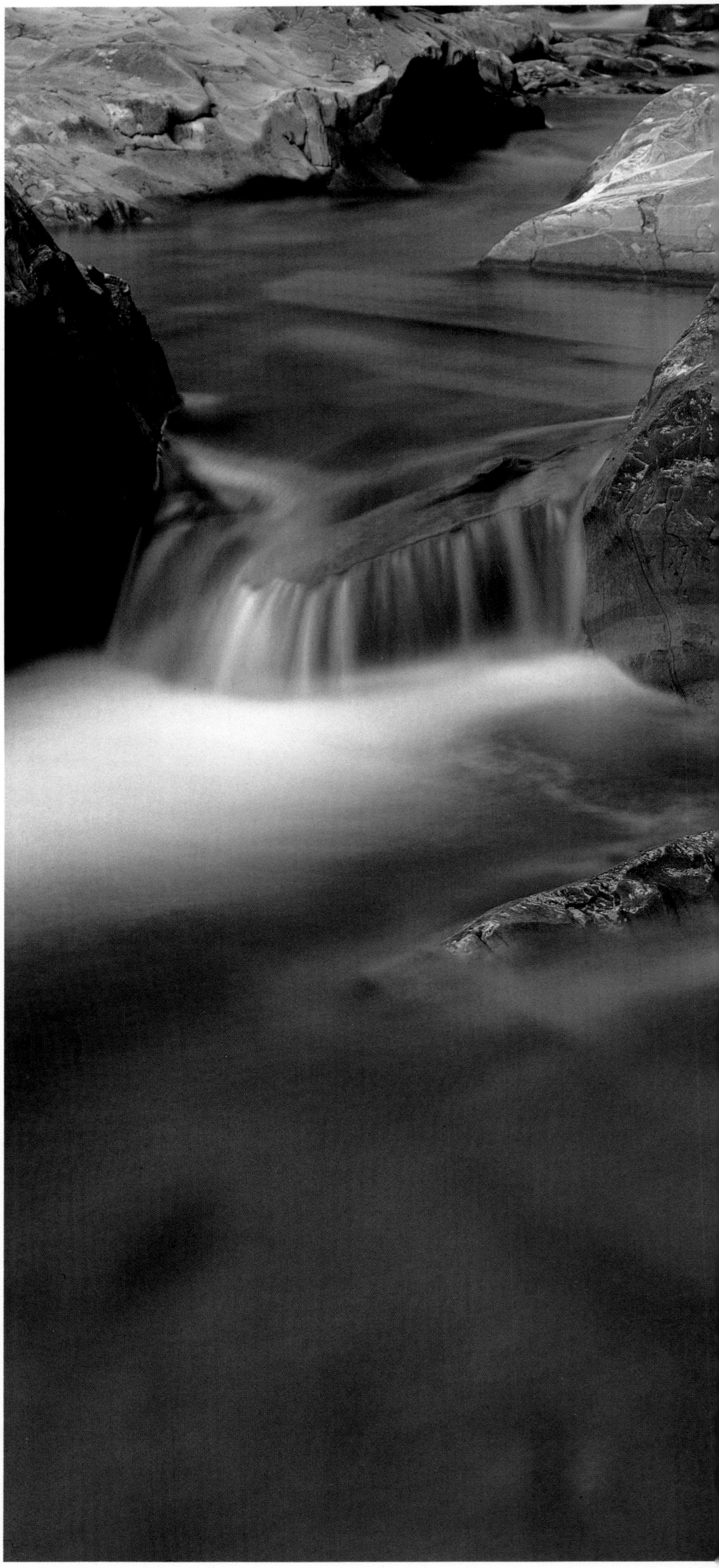

——— 1
——— 2
——— 0

1
2
2

1 ——
2 ——
3 ——

Photographs from Georg Stefan Troller's book "Paris – Ein Merian Buch".

Photographies du livre de Georg Stefan Troller "Paris – Ein Merian Buch" (Paris – Un livre Merian).

Photos aus Georg Stefan Trollers Buch "Paris – Ein Merian Buch".

Pages 123 to 125

Hartmut Brückner
Designer · Maquettiste · Gestalter

Max Scheler
Art Director · Directeur Artistique · Art Direktor

Hoffmann und Campe Verlag
Publisher · Editeur · Verleger

1
2
4

1
2
6

Rik Comello
Designer · Maquettiste · Gestalter

Photograph taken without the use of montage, which appeared in the Ptt-Jaarverslag annual in Holland.

Photographie prise sans l'utilisation de montage, qui a paru dans l'annuaire Ptt-Jaarverslag en Hollande.

Photo, aufgenommen ohne Montage und erschienen im Ptt-Jaarverslag Jahrbuch in Holland.

Cover photograph for the book "Kijkwerk," which was published in Holland, April 1983.

Photographie de couverture du livre "Kijkwerk," qui a été publié en Hollande, avril 1983.

Titel-Photo für das Buch "Kijkwerk," veröffentlicht in Holland im April 1983.

Photographs from the book "English Cottages" by Tony Evans and Candida Lycett Green.

Photographies du livre "English Cottages" (Petites maisons de campagne anglaises) par Tony Evans et Candida Lycett Green.

Photos aus dem Buch "English Cottages" (Englische Landhäuser) von Tony Evans und Candida Lycett Green.

Hans Bockting/Rik Comello
Designers · Maquettistes · Gestalter

Rik Comello
Art Director · Directeur Artistique · Art Direktor

Pages 128 to 131

John Gorham
Designer · Maquettiste · Gestalter

Weidenfeld & Nicolson
Publisher · Editeur · Verleger

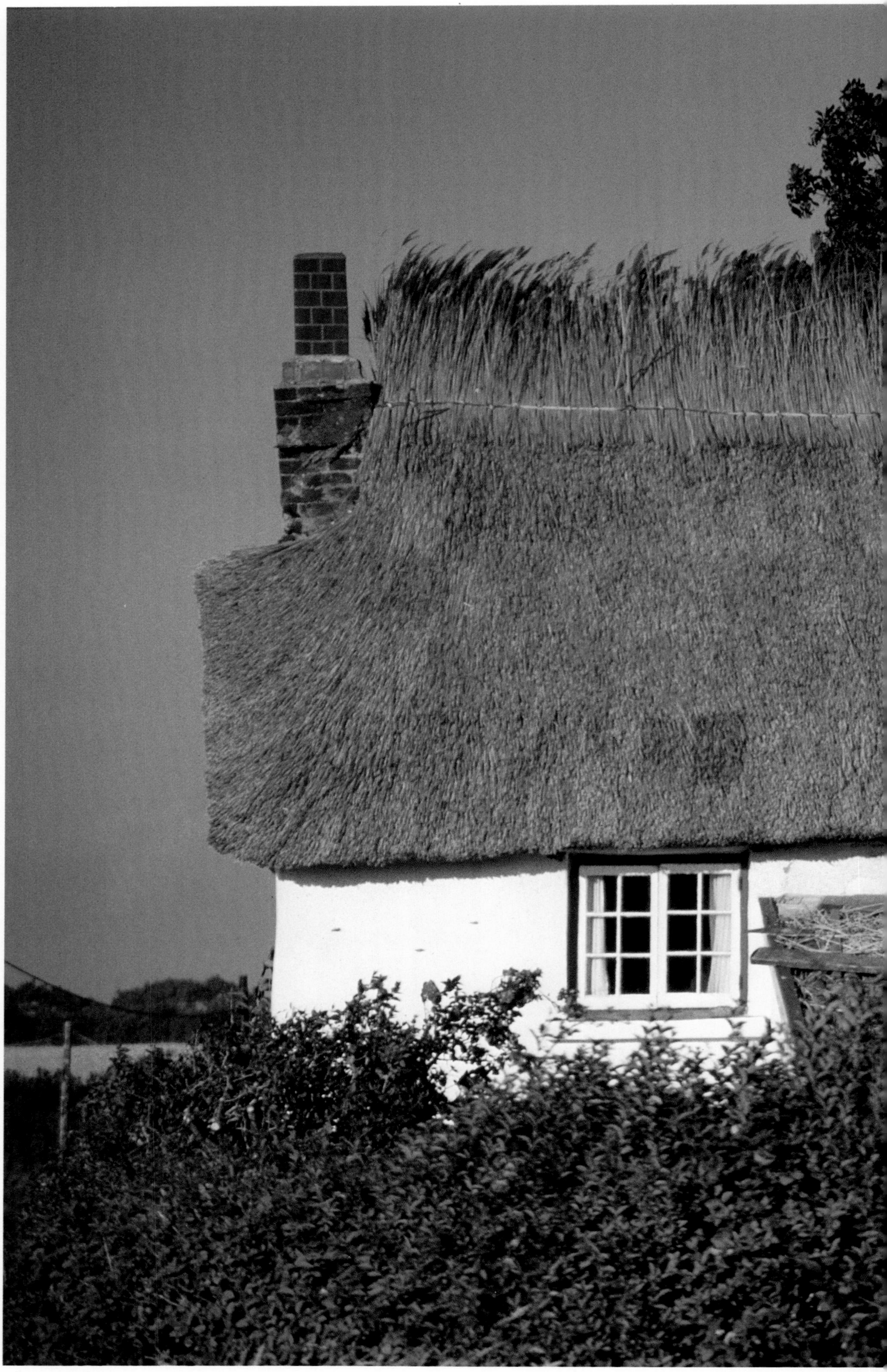

1
3
1

1
3
2

Jennie Burns
Designer · Maquettiste · Gestalter

Photograph of wasp's nests for a 1983 calendar, "Patterns in Nature."

Photographie de nids de guêpes pour un calendrier 1983, "Patterns in Nature" (Modèles dans la Nature).

Photo eines Wespennests für einen Kalender 1983, "Patterns in Nature" (Muster in der Natur).

Photograph taken in Essex for a record cover.

Photographie prise dans l'Essex pour une manche de disque.

Photo für eine Plattenhülle, aufgenommen in Essex.

1
3
6

John Merriman
Art Director · Directeur Artistique · Art Direktor

Collett Dickenson Pearce & Partners
Advertising Agency · Agence de Publicité · Werbeagentur

Alex Gunningham
Copywriter · Rédacteur · Texter

Gallaher Limited
Client · Client · Auftraggeber

Advertisement for Benson & Hedges which appeared in
various consumer magazines and theatre programmes.

Publicité pour Benson & Hedges qui a paru dans divers
magazines de consommation et programmes de théâtre.

Anzeige für Benson & Hedges, erschienen in verschiedenen
Verbraucherzeitschriften und Theaterprogrammen.

Advertisement for home insurance with the copyline "I don't have a lot of windows, so I only want to insure my contents," which appeared in the Dutch press.

Publicité pour assurance immobilière avec la légende "I don't have a lot of windows, so I only want to insure my contents" (Je n'ai pas beaucoup de fenêtres, alors je ne veux assurer que le contenu) qui a paru dans la presse hollandaise.

Anzeige für Hausversicherung mit dem Text "Ich habe nicht viele Fenster, deshalb will ich nur mein Hausgut versichern," erschienen in der holländischen Presse.

Marien de Goffau
Art Director · Directeur Artistique · Art Direktor

McCann-Erickson (Netherlands) BV
Advertising Agency · Agence de Publicité · Werbeagentur

Arie Klein
Copywriter · Rédacteur · Texter

Ennia NV
Client · Client · Auftraggeber

Photograph of the Conway Valley, with the copyline "The Conway Valley before and after the Shell pipeline," used for posters throughout the United Kingdom.

Photographie de la vallée Conway, avec la légende "The Conway Valley before and after the Shell pipeline" (La Vallée Conway avant et après l'oléoduc Shell) utilisée pour des affiches à travers tout le Royaume-Uni.

Photo des Conway Tales, mit dem Text "The Conway Valley before and after the Shell pipeline" (Das Conway Tal vor und nach der Shell Ölleitung), erschienen auf Plakaten überall in Großbritannien.

Pages 138, 139

Gary Horner
Art Director · Directeur Artistique · Art Direktor

Ogilvy Mather Limited
Advertising Agency · Agence de Publicité · Werbeagentur

Indra Sinhe
Copywriter · Rédacteur · Texter

Shell UK Limited
Client · Client · Auftraggeber

1
4
2

Advertisements for leather-wear which appeared in "Stern" in 1982.

Publicités pour vêtements de cuir qui ont parues dans "Stern" en 1982.

Anzeigen für Lederkleidung, erschienen im "Stern", 1982.

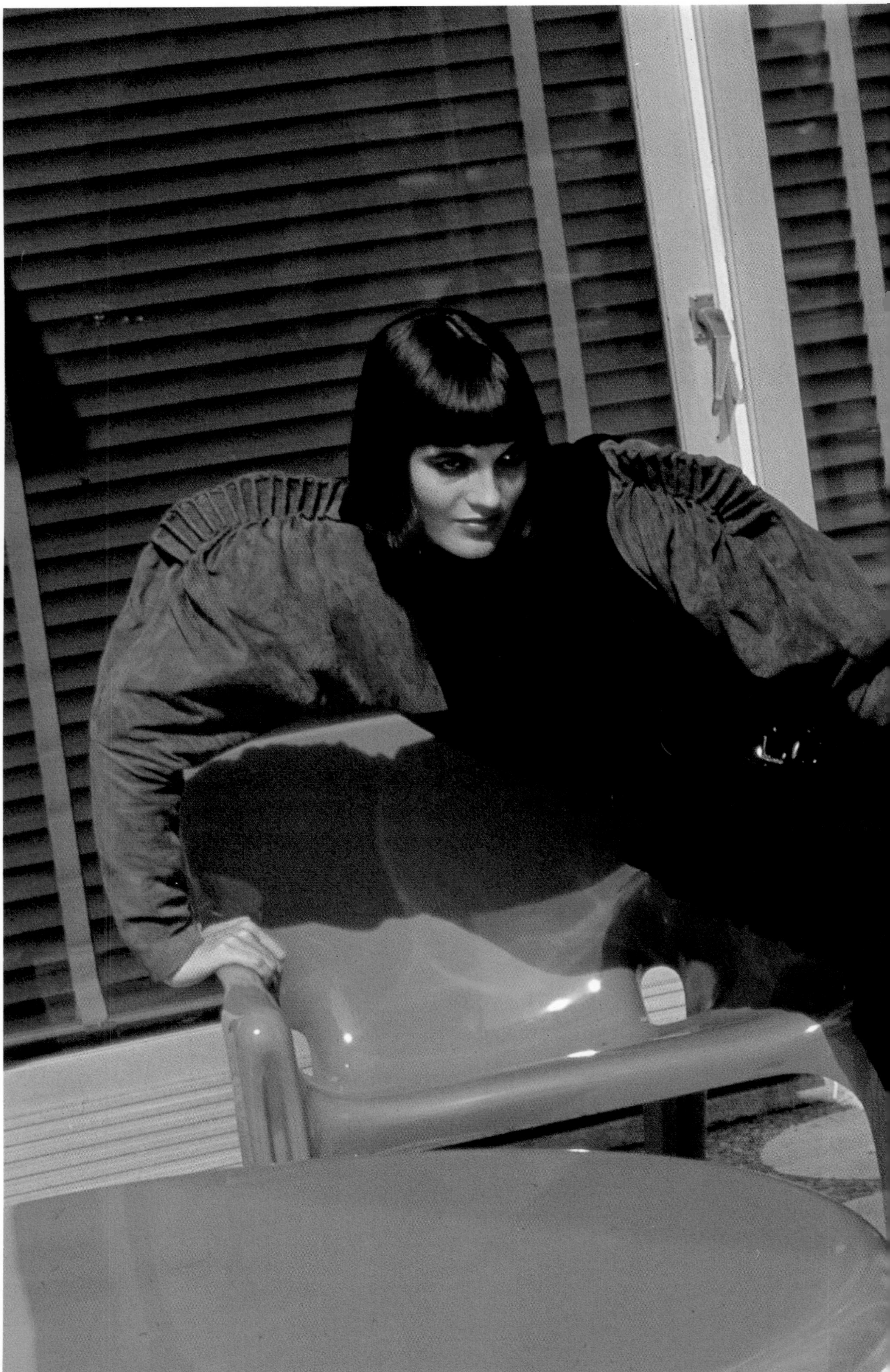

Nigel Rose
Art Director · Directeur Artistique · Art Direktor

Lynda McDonnell
Copywriter · Rédacteur · Texter

Collett Dickenson Pearce & Partners
Advertising Agency · Agence de Publicité · Werbeagentur

Gallaher Limited
Client · Client · Auftraggeber

Advertisement for Benson & Hedges which appeared on
posters and in the press.

Publicité pour Benson & Hedges qui a paru sur les affiches et
dans la presse.

Anzeige für Benson & Hedges, erschienen auf Plakaten und in
der Presse.

1 ——

4 ——

7 ——

Advertisement for Benson & Hedges Gold Box, which
appeared in various British magazines.

Tina Morgan
Art Director · Directeur Artistique · Art Direktor

Publicité pour Benson & Hedges Gold Box, qui a paru dans
divers magazines britanniques.

John Pallant
Copywriter · Rédacteur · Texter

Anzeige für Benson & Hedges Gold Box, erschienen in
verschiedenen britischen Zeitschriften.

Gallaher Limited
Client · Client · Auftraggeber

1
4
8

Paul Arden/Andy Rott
Art Directors · Directeurs Artistiques · Art Direktoren

Advertisement for "The Daily Mail" newspaper which
appeared in "Campaign," May 1983.

Mark Williams
Copywriter · Rédacteur · Texter

Publicité pour le journal "The Daily Mail" qui a paru dans
"Campaign," mai 1983.

Saatchi & Saatchi
Advertising Agency · Agence de Publicité · Werbeagentur

Anzeige für die Zeitung "The Daily Mail," erschienen in
"Campaign," Mai 1983.

Daily Mail Newspapers Limited
Client · Client · Auftraggeber

Advertisement for "The Daily Mail" newspaper which appeared in "Campaign", November 1982.

Paul Arden
Art Director · Directeur Artistique · Art Direktor

Publicité pour le journal "The Daily Mail" qui a paru dans "Campaign", novembre 1982.

Simon Dicketts
Copywriter · Rédacteur · Texter

Anzeige für die Zeitung "The Daily Mail", erschienen in "Campaign", November 1982.

Saatchi & Saatchi
Advertising Agency · Agence de Publicité · Werbeagentur

Bela Stamenkovits
Art Director · Directeur Artistique · Art Direktor

Hans van Waalbeek
Copywriter · Rédacteur · Texter

Prins Meyer Stamenkovits Van Walbeek
Advertising Agency · Agence de Publicité · Werbeagentur

Douwe Egberts
Client · Client · Auftraggeber

Advertisements for instant coffee which appeared in
magazines in Holland during the summer of 1982.

Publicités pour le café en poudre qui ont paru dans des
magazines en Hollande pendant l'été de 1982.

Anzeigen für Pulverkaffee, erschienen in Zeitschriften in
Holland im Sommer 1982.

1
5
2

Graham Fink Art Director · Directeur Artistique · Art Direktor	Advertisement for Benson & Hedges which appeared on posters and in the press.
Steve Limbrick Copywriter · Rédacteur · Texter	Publicité pour Benson & Hedges qui a paru sur les affiches et dans la presse.
Collett Dickenson Pearce & Partners Advertising Agency · Agence de Publicité · Werbeagentur	Anzeige für Benson & Hedges, erschienen auf Plakaten und in der Presse.
Gallaher Limited Client · Client · Auftraggeber	

1
5
3

Photograph of "The George & Dragon" in Lancashire with a cricket team, used as a poster advertising Tetley Bitter with the copyline "You can't beat 'em".

Photographie de "The George & Dragon" dans le Lancashire avec une équipe de cricket, utilisée comme affiche de publicité par Tetley Bitter avec la légende "You can't beat 'em" (Impossible de les battre).

Photo des Pubs "The George & Dragon" in Lancashire mit einem Kricket-Team, eingesetzt für ein Werbeplakat für Tetley Bitter mit dem Text "You can't beat 'em" (Die sind nicht zu schlagen).

Peter Vincent
Art Director · Directeur Artistique · Art Direktor

Kirkwood & Company Limited
Advertising Agency · Agence de Publicité · Werbeagentur

Allied Breweries
Client · Client · Auftraggeber

1
5
4

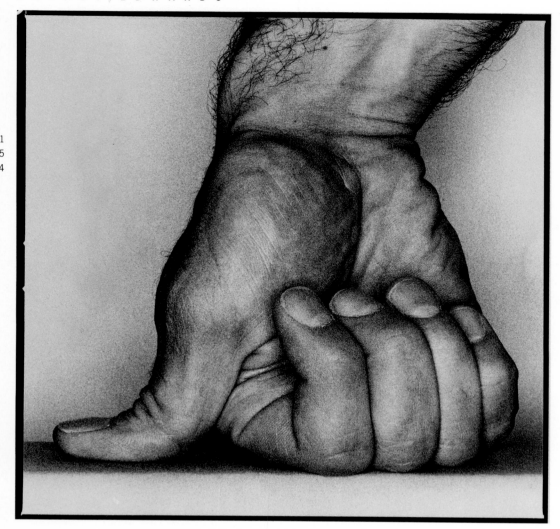

Tony Kaye
Art Director · Directeur Artistique · Art Direktor

Collett Dickenson Pearce & Partners
Advertising Agency · Agence de Publicité · Werbeagentur

Barclays Bank Limited
Client · Client · Auftraggeber

Photograph which was part of the "Man under Thumb" advertisement for Barclays Bank, which appeared in British newspapers.

Photographie qui faisait partie de la publicité pour Barclays Bank "Man under Thumb" (Homme sous le pouce), qui a paru dans les journaux britanniques.

Photo innerhalb der Anzeige "Man under Thumb" (Mann unter dem Daumen) für Barclays Bank, erschienen in britischen Zeitungen.

Poster used throughout the London area, with the headline "Rush Hour in Milton Keynes."

Affiche utilisée dans toute la région de Londres, ayant pour titre "Rush hour in Milton Keynes" (Heure de pointe à Milton Keynes).

Plakat, eingesetzt im Londoner Bereich, mit dem Titel "Rush hour in Milton Keynes" (Stoßzeit in Milton Keynes).

Mike Murphy
Art Director · Directeur Artistique · Art Direktor

Cogent Elliott
Advertising Agency · Agence de Publicité · Werbeagentur

Paul White
Copywriter · Rédacteur · Texter

Milton Keynes Development Corporation
Client · Client · Auftraggeber

Advertisement for Benson & Hedges which appeared in various colour supplements in November 1982.

Publicité pour Benson & Hedges qui a paru dans divers suppléments en couleurs en novembre 1982.

Anzeige für Benson & Hedges, erschienen in verschiedenen Farbbeilagen im November 1982.

Pages 156, 157

Nigel Rose
Art Director · Directeur Artistique · Art Direktor

Collett Dickenson Pearce & Partners
Advertising Agency · Agence de Publicité · Werbeagentur

Gallaher Limited
Client · Client · Auftraggeber

1
5
6

Couleurs
extra fines
à l'huile
CARRETIER
PARIS
LAQUE
GERANIUM
ROUGE DE
SATURNE
VERT DE
COBALT CLAI

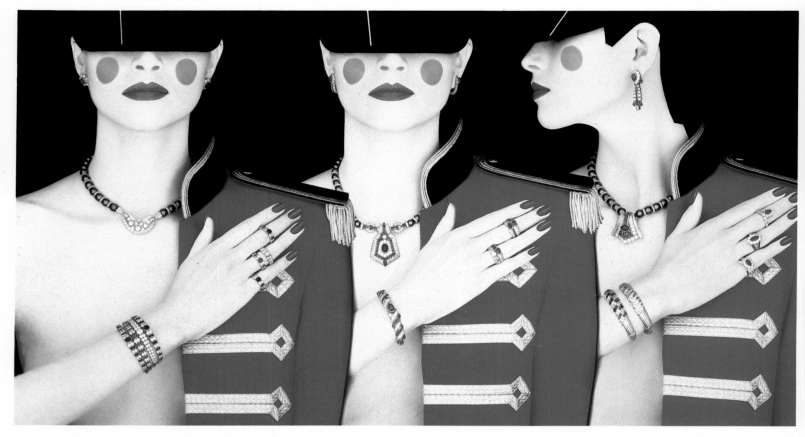

Ted Vaughan
Art Director · Directeur Artistique · Art Direktor

Lansdowneuro
Advertising Agency · Agence de Publicité · Werbeagentur

Tom Gattos
Copywriter · Rédacteur · Texter

Graff Diamonds
Client · Client · Auftraggeber

Advertisement for jewellery with the copyline "Unmistakably Graff" which appeared in "Vogue," "The Tatler" and "Harpers."

Publicité pour de la bijouterie avec la légende "Unmistakably Graff" (Manifestement Graff) qui a paru dans "Vogue," "The Tatler" et "Harpers."

Anzeige für Juwelen mit dem Text "Unmistakably Graff" (Unverkennbar Graff), erschienen in "Vogue," "The Tatler" und "Harpers."

Photograph with the copyline "Our Colour Range used to be as wide as Henry Ford's," used on an in-store poster for Ilfochrome 100.

Photographie avec la légende "Our Colour Range used to be as wide as Henry Ford's" (Notre éventail de couleurs était aussi large que celui de Henry Ford) utilisée sur une affichette intérieur pour Ilfochrome 100.

Photo mit dem Text "Our Colour Range used to be as wide as Henry Ford's" (Unsere Farbpalette war einstmals so breit wie die von Henry Ford", eingesetzt in Einzelhandels– plakaten für Ilfochrome 100.

Simon Minchin
Art Director · Directeur Artistique · Art Direktor

F.C.O. Univas Limited
Advertising Agency · Agence de Publicité · Werbeagentur

Derek Payne
Copywriter · Rédacteur · Texter

Ilford Limited
Client · Client · Auftraggeber

1 ——
6 ——
1 ——

Unpublished still-life photograph of lillies in a vase.

Photographie non publiée d'une nature morte de lis dans un vase.

Unveröffentlichtes Stilleben-Photo von Lilien in einer Vase.

1 ——
6 ——
3 ——

Unpublished still life photographs of tulips.   Pages 163 to 165

Photographies non publiées de natures-mortes aux tulipes.

Unveröffentlichte Stilleben-Photos von Tulpen.

Pages 166 to 169   Unpublished photographs taken in Venice.

Photographies non publiées prises à Venise.

Unveröffentlichte Photos, aufgenommen in Venedig.

1 ———
6 ———
7 ———

1
6
9

Unpublished photograph of a "stone field," taken on location in
Mauritius.

Photographie non publiée d'un "champ de pierres" prise en
extérieur à l'Ile Maurice.

Unveröffentlichtes Photo eines "Steinfeldes," aufgenommen in
Mauritius.

Unpublished photographs taken on location in England.

Photographies non publiées prises en extérieur en Angleterre.

Unveröffentlichte Photos aufgenommen in England.

Unpublished photographs taken on location in Greece.

Photographies non publiées prises en extérieur en Grèce.

Unveröffentlichte Photos aufgenommen in Griechenland.

None

1
7
3

1
7
4

Pages 174, 175   Unpublished photographs taken on location in England.

Photographies non publiées prises en extérieur en Angleterre.

Unveröffentlichte Photos aufgenommen in England.

1
7
5

Unpublished photograph of Loch Awe in Scotland.   Page 176, 177

Photographie non publiée du Loch Awe en Ecosse.

Unveröffentlichtes Photo des Loch Awe in Schottland.

Unpublished photograph of Mount Etna in Sicily.

Photographie non publiée du Mont Etna en Sicile.

Unveröffentlichtes Photo des Ätna in Sizilien.

Unpublished photograph taken from the beach in Atlantic City,
U.S.A. The 'glowing' building is the Playboy Club.

Photographie non publiée prise de la place à Atlantic City,
U.S.A. Le bâtiment 'luisant' est le Playboy Club.

Unveröffentlichtes Photo, aufgenommen vom Strand in
Atlantic City, U.S.A. Das 'strahlende' Gebäude ist der Playboy
Club.

Unpublished photograph taken for the publicity campaign run
by "Crédit Agricole" in France.

Photographie non publiée prise pour une campagne de publicité
organisée par "Crédit Agricole" en France.

Unveröffentlichtes Photo, aufgenommen für eine Publicity-
Kampagne der "Crédit Agricole" in Frankreich.

Unpublished photograph taken in Venice.

Photographie non publiée prise à Venise.

Unveröffentlichtes Photo, aufgenommen in Venedig.

Unpublished photographs taken while travelling through the
People's Republic of China.

Photographies non publiées prises au cours d'un voyage à
travers la République Populaire de Chine.

Unveröffentlichte Photos, aufgenommen auf einer Reise durch
die Volksrepublik China.

Unpublished photograph of Kit Williams for a feature
"Masquerade – Final Riddle" by Susan Raven in "The Sunday
Times Magazine."

Photographie non publiée de Kit Williams pour un article
"Masquerade – Final Riddle" (Mascarade – La dernière énigme)
par Susan Raven dans "The Sunday Times Magazine."

Unveröffentlichtes Photo von Kit Williams für den Artikel
"Masquerade – Final Riddle" (Maskerade – das letzte Rätsel)
von Susan Raven in "The Sunday Times Magazine."

Unpublished photograph of an Essex wheatfield taken during
a thunderstorm.

Photographie non publiée d'un champ de blé dans l'Essex
prise pendant un orage.

Univeröffentlichtes Photo eines Weizenfeldes in Essex,
aufgenommen während eines Gewitters.

■